PREPARING AMERICA'S TEACHERS

by DONALD R. CRUICKSHANK

and Associates

DEBORAH BAINER

JOSUÉ CRUZ, JR.

CARMEN GIEBELHAUS

JOY D. McCULLOUGH

KIM KENNETH METCALF

RICHARD REYNOLDS

Published by
Phi Delta Kappa Educational Foundation

Cover design by Peg Caudell

Library of Congress Catalog Card Number 96-68562
ISBN 0-87367-486-3
Copyright © 1996 by Donald R. Cruickshank
Bloomington, Indiana U.S.A.

This book is dedicated to two of my mentors, E.C. "Pete" Merrill and Bob Howsam. Together they facilitated my appreciation and understanding of many things.

Donald R. Cruickshank

$\mathcal{A}$CKNOWLEDGMENTS

My several co-authors provided assistance as follows:

Chapter 1, Joy McCullough, Director of Teacher Education, Trinity Western University, British Columbia.

Chapter 2, Carmen Giebelhaus, Assistant Professor, University of Dayton.

Chapter 3, Kim Metcalf, Director of the Teacher Education Laboratory, Indiana University, and Deborah Bainer, Associate Professor, Ohio State University.

Chapter 4, Richard Reynolds, Assistant Professor, Eastern Connecticut University, and Josué Cruz, Jr., Professor, University of South Florida.

Liz Rhyner prepared the manuscript.

$\mathcal{T}$ABLE OF CONTENTS

*I*NTRODUCTION

Because Americans venerate education, it comes as no surprise that this enterprise is inspected and criticized regularly and that educators are expected to respond to these criticisms. And when the critics believe that those responses have not resulted in the highest possible standards, the criticism is especially sharp. In any case, teachers and the way in which they are prepared usually are depicted as villains.

There are many recurrent criticisms of teacher preparation. Among them are: students enrolled in colleges of education are intellectually inferior; the curriculum in colleges of education is impoverished, often redundant, and remote from the challenges facing K-12 schools; education faculty give their teaching too little attention, do not model what is known about effective teaching, produce routine and often ill-conceived scholarship, and stay away from public school classrooms; and teacher preparation programs seldom are evaluated in terms of the teaching ability of their graduates.

Sykes (1983) referred to teacher preparation as the "imperiled profession." In the last decade, it has become further endangered by continued reduction of its already scarce fiscal resources, rollbacks in curriculum, its attempted elimination as an undergraduate major, the proliferation of alternative routes to certification, and recruitment of disillusioned or retired workers from other fields as prospective teachers. In addition, there is increasing criticism from within the ranks of teacher preparation.

1

In the midst of all this criticism, teacher educators have to continue to perform their most important role, which is to prepare the best teachers for America's schools. Fortunately, there are at least three factors supporting the work of teacher educators. The first is a strong, if imperfect, curricular tradition, which we call the "modal curriculum." In addition to this tradition, there also is a large number of ideas for improving the curriculum. And third, teacher educators have many ways in which the curriculum can be communicated or delivered.

With knowledge of the criticisms, an abundance of reform ideas, and an understanding and willingness to overcome numerous obstacles, we should be able to move teacher preparation toward a brighter future.

References

Sykes, G. "Contradictions, Ironies, and Promises Unfulfilled: A Contemporary Account of the Status of Teaching." *Phi Delta Kappan* 65 (October 1983): 87-93.

Chapter 1
$\mathcal{T}$HE MODAL TEACHER
PREPARATION CURRICULUM

Since 1839, when Horace Mann declared that teachers require special preparation, a debate has raged over how American teachers should be prepared. Indeed, not all critics have agreed with Mann's early assertion that teachers require special preparation. Even some of those who do agree believe that only a little preparation is adequate. There has been a constant tug-of-war between those who believe that teachers need most to be well-educated persons with a solid background in the academic subjects they will teach and others who believe that, in addition, there is a body of knowledge related to teaching and learning that will enhance teacher performance and student achievement.

This struggle has resulted in the variety of reform proposals noted in Chapter 2 of this book. The struggle is most visible on university campuses, where periodic arguments occur between academicians, who seek to reduce the professional education coursework of education majors, and the much smaller professional education faculty. The "war" also is visible in state governments, where some legislatures recently have taken the position that more general education and less special, professional education is better.

Some professional educators have argued for changing the curriculum so that both sides win. That is done by extending the teacher preparation curriculum to five or six years (AACTE 1982, 1993; Carnegie Forum 1986; Goodlad 1990; Holmes Group 1986; Smith 1980; Wisniewski 1989). However, few universities have extended programs; and teacher preparation remains primarily an undergraduate activity (Wong and Osguthorpe 1993).

The curriculum for preservice teachers usually is divided into either three or four parts, depending on the nomenclature that teacher educators choose to use. The three basic segments are general education, content or subject matter related to the teaching specialty, and pedagogy, or knowledge of the art and science of teaching. When divided into four parts, pedagogy is split into two, the knowledge of education practice and skill in the practice of teaching. For example, the National Association of State Directors of Teacher Education and Certification prefers to divide teacher education into three parts, their terms being 1) general education, 2) teaching major or field of specialization, and 3) professional education (NASDTEC 1989). On the other hand, the National Council for the Accreditation of Teacher Education (NCATE 1995) describes four aspects: 1) general studies, 2) content studies, 3) professional/pedagogical studies, and 4) integrative studies.

Since the majority of teachers are prepared in colleges and universities seeking NCATE accreditation or endorsement, we will use NCATE's nomenclature. Briefly, *general studies* refers to the study of subjects and ideas purported to be of value to all persons. *Content studies* refers to the study of content in the academic area in which the preservice teacher plans to teach and to the study of how to teach that content. *Professional and pedagogical studies* pertains to the study of what teachers should know about teaching and learning, while *integrative studies* refers to "putting it all together" during what normally are called on- and off-campus clinical and laboratory experiences. In this chapter, the four parts of the modal, or most common, teacher preparation curriculum are examined.

General Studies

The Harvard Committee on General Education (1945) introduced the term "general education" to describe a curriculum that is designed to prepare an individual to be a free person and citizen. The curriculum that would contribute to these ends was said to consist of the natural sciences (understanding of the physical environment and human beings' relationship to it), the social sciences (understanding of the social environment and human beings' relationship to it), and the humanities (understanding of human beings themselves in their evolution and ways of thinking).

At most universities, the general education curriculum still follows the notions contained in the Harvard Committee Report and consists of courses in the social sciences, natural sciences, and humanities. However, according to Silberman (1970), such courses all too often are taught with a narrowly professional or technical purpose in mind and are designed to train professional historians, mathematicians, physicists, and so forth. In fact, general education requirements for undergraduates on most campuses usually are not very specific. That is, rather than prescriptions for exact course requirements, there are only general stipulations. Many universities readily admit that they do not offer anything resembling a true general education. Instead, they refer to their requirements simply as basic education requirements.

The demise of true general education on university campuses has been attributed to many things, including lack of interest on the part of students. Sewall (1982) asks:

> Do the liberal studies — that is, the bodies of knowledge that include language, mathematics, science, history, civics and the fine arts — still possess enough authority to capture the imagination of young people easily diverted by more sensate activities? Could yet another generation largely indifferent to mental exertion and precision inflict irreparable damage on a citizen-propelled polity and an information-based economy? Should we brace ourselves for a plague of cultural amnesia? (p. 603)

General education also has been hurt by two other factors. First, employers in business and industry lack interest in supporting general education. And second, university faculty, who operate under a reward system based on research and publications, have lost interest in teaching undergraduates.

5

A number of arguments support the proposition that teachers must be generally well educated. For example, there is a commonly held expectation that because they are responsible for the formal general education of K-12 students, teachers must have a similarly strong background themselves. They need to draw easily and regularly on this background to enrich the education of their students. In addition, teachers serve as role models for students, each other, and the community (AACTE 1985). Conant (1963) amplifies:

> There is, moreover, an important practical reason for certain studies; almost any teacher inevitably faces the necessity of dealing with subjects outside his area of specialization, not only in his classroom but also in conversation with students. If he is largely ignorant or uninformed, he can do much harm. Moreover, if the teachers in a school system are to be a group of learned persons cooperating together, they should have as much intellectual experience in common as possible, and any teacher who has not studied in a variety of fields in college will always feel far out of his depth when talking with a colleague who is the high school teacher in a field other than his own.
>
> And too, if teachers are to be considered as learned persons in their communities (as they are in certain European countries), and if they are to command the respect of the professional men and women they meet, they must be prepared to discuss difficult topics. This requires a certain level of sophistication. For example, to participate in any but the most superficial conversations about the impact of science in our culture, one must have at some time wrestled with the problems of the theory of knowledge. The same is true when it comes to the discussion of current issues (pp. 93-94).

The importance of general education for teachers is acknowledged by the National Council for the Accreditation of Teacher Education (NCATE), the National Association of State Directors of Teacher Education and Certification (NASDTEC), and all state departments of education.

Four decades ago, NCATE stated its position on the importance of general education for teachers:

> Ideally . . . all persons in our society should be well-edu-
> cated. For the teacher, however, being well-educated is a
> necessity. Without it, the teacher cannot interpret any field
> of knowledge in its proper relationship to the whole of soci-
> ety, and without it, the teacher will not be respected by a
> society which is itself becoming increasingly well-educated.
> . . . The committee believes . . . that being a well-educated
> person is so essential to the satisfactory performance of the
> functions of a teacher at all levels as to justify an emphasis
> on liberal education at the preservice level. (Armstrong
> 1957, p. 9)

Since that time, the importance of general education as a component of teacher education has been reinforced regularly in NCATE
standards for national accreditation and NASDTEC standards for
state program approval. The most recent NCATE standards (1995)
call for courses in arts, communication, history, literature, mathematics, philosophy, sciences, and the social sciences. The standards
note that these courses should be taught "with emphasis upon gen-
eralization rather than the academic specialization as a primary
objective" (p. 15) and that they should incorporate multicultural
and global perspectives. NCATE recommends that these courses
should be completed in the first two or three years of a four-year
program.

Earlier NCATE standards (1982) indicate that general education
should constitute a minimum of one-third of the total coursework
of future teachers. According to Parker (1993), in the approximately 1,300 teacher education programs studied, including both
four- and five-year programs, two-thirds of a student's program is
in arts and sciences and one-third is in professional education
with a culminating student teaching experience. Secondary teachers may take more arts and science courses in their teaching
fields.

While there is support for the general education of teachers,
there are concerns about what general education has become in
practice. According to B.O. Smith:

> Schools of pedagogy no less than the nonpedagogical
> schools and departments have been, and continue to be, pos-

7

sessed by the magic of the expression "general education." The referent even in the most stringent definitions is elusive. Its meanings are as numerous as the points of view regarding what education is all about. To some it means dipping into a number of disciplines, tasting general courses here and there; to others it means pursuing a program in the humanities which strangely enough often skirts philosophy, the integrative discipline par excellence.

As a result of preoccupation with the notion of general education, a considerable proportion of the prospective teacher's academic program, sometimes amounting to half of the credit hours, has been distributed over a large number of fields from which the student has acquired only very superficial knowledge. (1980, pp. 31-32)

Ritsch argues that what teachers need from a liberal arts education and what professors in the liberal arts teach often are at odds:

I suggest that education has as a necessary function in the preparation of teachers the constant application of the processes of thinking and activities of understanding to the form and substance of the liberal arts disciplines. Certainly a primary aim of teachers is the communication of the availability, place, meanings, and values of those knowledges which are the foci of liberal arts disciplines to those who have had little or no contact with these disciplines as areas of significant human knowledge. Thus, education must, in the training of teachers, demand that prospective teachers come to grips with such basic questions as: "What does this or that particular area of knowledge mean?" "What basic sets of questions and historical context gave rise to this or that particular area of concentrated knowledge, and what is the place of this or that concentrated knowledge today?" "What methods, skills, and value concerns have resulted from the shaping and elaboration of this or that discipline, and how do these relate to other disciplines or areas of knowledge?" All such questions lead toward such fundamental concerns of teacher preparation as "How and when do I, as a teacher, go about preparing students to comprehend and then undertake studies in this or that area of knowledge?" and "What do these disciplines or areas of knowledge have to offer that might improve efforts to teach, contribute to learning, and improve understanding of the social, historical, and philosophical contexts of schooling?" These are, for the most part, questions which are not central to the concerns of the liberal arts professors, yet which are, or should be, vital concerns of the prospective teacher, especially elementary and middle school teachers. (1981, pp. 408-409)

A smaller number of academicians believe that possession of a general education should be the *sole* criterion for entry into teaching. Mortimer Adler (1982) calls for a single-track system of public education that provides all children, K-12, with the same curriculum with virtually no electives and no vocational training. That curriculum would consist of fundamental knowledge (history, literature, language, mathematics, science, and fine arts), basic intellectual skills (reading, writing, mathematical computation, and scientific investigation), and the enlargement of understanding (aesthetic appreciation of works of art, ability to think critically). In addition, Adler proposes 12 years of physical education, eight years of varied manual arts (cooking, typing, auto repair), and at least one year focusing on choosing a career. Since the Paideia curriculum contains the "general learning that should be the possession of all human beings," Adler proposes that its teachers must receive a solid liberal arts education and "the hell with courses in pedagogy and educational philosophy" (Stengel 1982).

Unfortunately, teachers sometimes have been viewed as not having even a basic education. An article in the 16 June 1980 issue of *Time*, "Help! Teachers Can't Teach!" is illustrative of how too many people view teachers.

> Quite a few teachers, estimates range to twenty percent, simply have not mastered the basic skills in reading, writing and arithmetic that they are supposed to teach. (p. 55)

Perhaps the public is correct. A study sponsored by the National Endowment for the Humanities (Galambos 1985) compared more than 3,283 education graduates and 2,760 arts and science graduates from 17 major universities in the South. It found teacher education graduates had a weaker general education curriculum, less coursework in each of the major academic areas of general education, and fewer upper-level liberal arts courses. Consequently, Galambos suggests that there is a need to bring the general education of teachers up to the "college" level.

Various states have announced their intention to ensure that teachers be well-educated persons, or at least be competent in the basics, by mandating teacher competency tests. For example, Florida requires teacher candidates to pass the Florida Teacher Certification Examination (Florida Department of Education 1982), which contains subtests in reading, writing, mathematics, and professional education. Oklahoma examines teacher candidates only in their major and minor approval areas. For example, a prospective teacher of algebra is examined both on algebra and on general mathematics. Many other states have bills pending that call for similar measures. In addition, many states have mandated that prior to admission to teacher education programs, candidates must demonstrate basic competencies as evidenced by scores on such standardized tests as the Scholastic Aptitude Test (SAT), the American College Testing Program Assessment Test (ACT), or the California Achievement Test (CAT) (Ward 1981).

In conclusion, the public, teacher educators, and academicians agree that teachers should be well educated. However, general education, and particularly the general education of teachers, suffers from neglect.

In order to improve the general education of teachers, the following questions need to be addressed. Can general education be redefined or reinterpreted in a way that has common acceptance and that will provide direction? How much general education is necessary relative to the total curriculum for teachers? What should constitute the general education curriculum for teachers? How can education students and faculty alike be drawn toward general education? How can teacher education accrediting and approval agencies be made more interested in the general education of teachers? How well are current preservice teachers being generally educated? Finally, are generally educated teachers more effective teachers?

Here are a few suggestions that may assist in the resolution of some problems related to general studies:

1. Ensure that all stakeholders in teacher preparation are acutely aware of the meaning, purpose, and importance of general studies.
2. Make certain that general studies courses that involve preservice teachers embody the spirit of general education.
3. Continue efforts to define the nature and scope of general studies and its role in teacher preparation. Teacher education scholars should be involved in this process.

Content Studies

No one would argue the need for teachers to know their subjects, and criticism is quick to follow those teachers who do not. However, having knowledge of a subject and competence in teaching it are two different qualities. In this regard, Feiman-Nemser (1990) notes:

> Teachers need more than content knowledge. They need a special blend of content and pedagogy that Shulman has labeled pedagogical content knowledge. The unique province of teachers, *pedagogical content knowledge* includes useful ways to conceptualize and represent commonly taught topics . . . plus understanding of what makes learning those topics difficult or easy for students of different ages and backgrounds. (p. 221)

All who have a stake in K-12 education uphold the principles that 1) teachers must know the content they will teach and 2) they must be aware of how best to teach it.

At issue, however, is how the second principle is accomplished. Before about 1950, when teachers colleges still existed, the academic faculty accepted the responsibility not only for teaching prospective science teachers knowledge of biology, chemistry, physics, and so on, but also for teaching them its essences and how best to help K-12 students understand and appreciate those things. That was done easily because all their students were prospective teachers. In contrast, science classes in today's multipurpose universities are populated by students from a variety of majors. In these situations, faculty have little time or inclination to instruct the few future teachers in "pedagogical content knowledge." Howsam and his colleagues note that problems arise because prospective teachers normally populate the same classes as other university students:

> academic faculty sometimes assume that when . . . education majors learn the research procedures, logic and content of an academic specialty their ability to . . . excite others about the value of the discipline will follow. Some of the faculty also assume that knowledge of a subject is sufficient preparation for teaching it. Courses designed primarily to meet the needs of majors who intend advanced graduate study often neglect the concerns of others, particularly teachers. (1976, pp. 85-86)

Perhaps future teachers will have to synthesize and integrate content knowledge obtained from one group of academic faculty with pedagogical knowledge obtained from teacher educators.

In addition to needing content mastery and knowledge of how to teach that content in K-12 settings, Broudy (1972) argues that teachers also must possess *knowledge to teach with*. For example, history teachers must know both the history they will teach and history writ large. In addition, they need to know other subjects from which they can draw. Thus history teachers would benefit from study of related literature, music, and art for periods about which they will teach.

Knowledge available in, and supportive of, the content or teaching specialty seems endless and appears increasingly so. Fortunately, there are criteria, albeit subjective, by which that content can be better selected: Is this the content that is taught in K-12 schools? Is this the content that will give the curriculum taught in the schools extended or enriched meaning? Is this the content that will help the preservice teacher understand and be able to communicate the discipline's attributes and ways of knowing?

Obviously, the kinds of persons who teach content to prospective teachers are critical. There several types of academic professors. One type is the academician whose major interest is to engage in scholarly research and to nurture students who will go to graduate school and major in the discipline. This type likely is not interested in teaching the subject specialty in such a way that it meets the needs of prospective teachers. A second type is the academician who, though not particularly interested in scholarship and preparing future graduate students, still treats all students as if they have the same purposes in studying that content area. A third type is the academician who has been given an additional responsibility for teacher preparation and therefore is sensitive, if not always responsive, to having preservice teachers as students. Finally, there are academic faculty, such as Nobel laureate physicist Kenneth Wilson, who have devoted much time and thought to the improved preparation of teachers (Wilson and Davis 1994).

There are persons other than academicians who are knowledgeable and competent to teach the content courses. They may be either members of the professional education faculty or practicing K-12 teachers. Clearly then, it depends on the motives of the persons teaching prospective teachers as to how they will approach the subject matter.

Academicians teaching content courses for teachers would be more sensitive to what preservice teachers need to know if they regularly interacted with K-12 teachers and teacher educators in their specialty area, or perhaps if they served on school district curriculum committees. Because most academicians teaching content courses for teachers do not maintain relationships with the schools or with teacher educators, they tend to be unaware of or insensitive to the needs of preservice teachers. Therefore, education departments have felt it necessary to continue to maintain special methods courses intended specifically to address both the content of a particular K-12 subject and how it should be taught.

A special word needs to be said about the content preparation of elementary teachers, because they teach all the so-called common-branch subjects. It is assumed that, because of their general education, prospective elementary teachers already know the content of the elementary school curriculum and need no further instruction. Results of teacher tests often deny such an assumption. Clearly, some preservice teachers must be taught or retaught the elementary content that they in turn will teach.

We would be hard-pressed to find university courses that provide content for or content to support the teaching fields of elementary teachers. An exception is a course in mathematics taught at Ohio State University, which purports "to develop basic ideas of arithmetic, algebra, and geometry as appropriate for elementary school teachers." There are no similar courses in science, literature, language arts, or social studies. The existence of this single course seems more of an indictment of the mathematics competency of elementary teachers than a course intended to enrich the content specialty.

Obtaining responses to the following questions might move us in the direction of improving delivery of content studies. What content do K-12 teachers need to know and be able to teach? Who should provide instruction to preservice teachers in the content studies? How can academic and professional education departments and K-12 schools become mutually supportive in this task?

Following are a few suggestions that may help to resolve some of the problems in this area of the curriculum:

1. Make the content courses that serve professional education students truly professional courses, rather than placing preservice teachers in courses intended as general education or as prerequisites for academic graduate study.
2. Define more clearly what should constitute the content for each teaching specialty, focusing on the needs of both elementary and secondary education.
3. Ensure that those academicians teaching content for teaching specialty courses are in contact with schools, teachers, and teacher educators.

4. Ensure that prospective teachers also are finding out how best to teach content to K-12 students.

Professional Education

If a primary criterion for any profession is that it possess a distinctive body of knowledge, then professional education would be "a specialized body of knowledge and skills . . . acquired during a prolonged period of education and training" (Schein 1972, p. 8). Such requisites obviously would differ among professions. In law, that knowledge is contained in courses on appellate practice, contracts, torts, and property. In medicine, professional knowledge and skills are gained in courses in cardiology, endocrinology, and pathophysiology. In education, such courses as tests and measurement, curriculum theory, and diagnosis of learning problems are offered. The essential common denominator of these courses is that generally they are not intended to be of particular interest or value to persons outside the profession.

Since Koerner's (1963) strong negative evaluation of education as an academic discipline 30 years ago, the field has moved to generate a significant knowledge base to undergird the preparation of teachers. That knowledge base now is becoming an integral part of the teacher preparation curriculum (AACTE 1991).

Perhaps the most serious obstacle preventing teaching from having true professional status is the lack of consensus among educators regarding what constitutes the requisite specialized body of knowledge and skills for effective teaching. For example, whereas a major Midwestern college of medicine lists more than 20 courses, individual studies, and seminars, the college of education in that university lists more than 300. Even accepting that the two fields are different and that education may be more inclusive and more diverse, surely medicine has more concurrence regarding a basic professional culture than does education.

Armstrong elaborates on the lack of consensus among teacher educators regarding a core professional culture:

> The lack of curriculum pattern indicates that the faculty
> of an institution has given no systematic thought to what

should be included in a teacher education program; that the faculty is unwilling to back its own judgment; or that it believes no pattern is necessary. Whatever the reason, it is likely to result in gaps in the academic and professional education taken by students, in undesirable over-lapping of content, in having students at different stages of their educational programs enrolled in the same courses, and in intensifying the problems of evaluation. (1957, p. 6)

Another obstacle interfering with education being perceived as a true profession is that a teacher's education is acquired mostly within a four-year undergraduate program, rather than during a prolonged period as with law and medicine. Over the past several decades, proposals have been put forth to extend preservice programs (Adler 1982; Carnegie Forum 1986; Holmes Group 1986; Smith 1980), but many of these encounter difficulties. The first difficulty already has been mentioned. The profession simply does not agree on what teachers must know to begin practice; therefore, there is no scope and sequence to curricula that would justify prolonged preparation.

A second difficulty is the belief on the part of many, including teacher educators, that prolonged preparation of teachers is not warranted economically. They ask, "Why would or should young people spend so much time and effort to become a teacher when the economic rewards are so low and there is a scarcity of available teaching positions?"

A third obstacle interfering with prolonged preparation is the historical division separating preservice and inservice education, now often called professional development.

Regardless of the professional status of teaching, most persons, including academicians, agree that teachers need to be professionally educated, for they alone are responsible for knowing formally how to educate others. Whitehead proclaims, "that the art and science of education require a study and genius of their own; and that this genius and this science are more than a bare knowledge of some branch of science or literature" (1949, p. 16). Silberman notes, "The question is not whether teachers should receive special preparation for teaching, but what kind of preparation they should receive" (1970, p. 413).

All states require that institutions preparing preservice teachers mandate that some coursework be taken in professional education. The disagreement occurs mostly over the nature and amount of the preservice education curriculum. Conant (1963), in his study of 77 institutions in 22 states, noted a few constants in teacher education curricula at that time, namely: educational psychology, at least one methods course, one course related to the function of the school in society, and student teaching. He reported that semester-hour professional course requirements for elementary majors ranged from 26 to 59 and for secondary majors from 17 to 30.

Chandler et al. (1971) estimated that about 15% of the work required for legal certification of high school teachers was devoted to the study of pedagogy and the practice of teaching under supervision. Similarly, they estimated the median for state certification for elementary teachers at 20%.

Sherwin (1974), in her study of 719 institutions, found the professional curriculum to be divided between psychological and social foundations and curriculum and instruction. Within the psychological and social foundations area, educational psychology was required most often. Sherwin reported that elementary majors had course requirements ranging from 26 to 35 semester hours.

As would be expected, teacher education accrediting and certification bodies mandate professional education for teachers. According to NCATE (1995), those abilities requisite to becoming a teacher can be subsumed under two categories: professional studies and pedagogical studies.

Professional studies refers to the historical, economic, sociological, philosophical, and psychological foundations of education. They more commonly are called "foundations of education" or "foundational studies in education." This component usually includes such courses as introduction to education, philosophy of education, history of education, educational psychology, educational sociology, educational anthropology, politics of education, economics of education, comparative education and, more recently, multicultural education, aesthetic education, and moral or ethical education. These courses are intended to serve as bridges between general education and pedagogy.

Although the Holmes Group report (1986) and the Carnegie Forum on Education and the Economy (1986) report largely ignore the role of these studies in teacher education (Borman 1990), several other sources support their inclusion in the preparation curriculum. The Council of Learned Societies in Education defines the role of educational foundations in teacher education programs, stating that these studies should be "broadly conceived" and "derive [their] character and fundamental theories from a number of academic disciplines, combinations of disciplines, and area studies: history, philosophy, sociology, anthropology, religion, political science, economics, psychology, comparative and international education, educational studies and educational policy studies" (1986, p. 3). Borman (1990) concurs that educational foundations courses can encourage both knowledge about current societal issues related to education and understanding of how these relate to classroom processes.

NCATE (1982) notes that there are certain issues in education that must be examined by considering their historical development and related philosophical, sociological, psychological, political, and religious aspects. These issues include the nature and aims of education; the curriculum, organization, and administration of a school system; and the processes of teaching and learning. NCATE's latest standards state that the professional studies component would enable students to acquire and learn to apply knowledge about:

> the social, historical, and philosophical foundations of education, including an understanding of the moral, social, and political dimensions of classrooms, teaching, and schools; the impact of technological and societal changes on schools, theories of human development and learning; inquiry and

research; school law and educational policy; professional ethics; and the responsibilities, structure, and activities of the profession. (NCATE 1995, p. 5)

Similarly, the National Association of State Directors of Teacher Education and Certification (NASDTEC) expects that:

The beginning teacher shall have completed a program that provides for the development of insights into child and adolescent psychology; the teaching-learning process; the social interactive process in the classroom, school and community . . . [and] the broader problems of the profession as they relate to society and the function of the schools. . . . The program shall require study of the leaders, ideas and movements underlying the development and organization of education in the U.S. (1989, pp. 12-13)

Some critics argue that the foundational studies should not be part of the professional education component of teacher education. Conant, for example, notes that such a component would be unnecessary if only "the general education of future teachers is well arranged." That being the case, "helpful philosophical, political and historical insights will be supplied by professors of philosophy, political science and history" (1963, p. 123). Conant advocates that preservice teachers should "study philosophy under a real philosopher. An additional course in philosophy of education would be desirable but not essential" (p. 131).

When Conant studied the education of American teachers, he found little semblance of rationality or unity in the content of foundations courses, stating, "Those in charge of these foundations courses often attempt to patch together scraps of history, philosophy, political theory, sociology and pedagogical ideology" (1963, p. 117). He referred to them as eclectic courses and advised their elimination, "for not only are they usually worthless, but they give education departments a bad name" (p. 117).

Broudy strongly disagrees with recommendations like Conant's, arguing that they are not practical.

Even the student who has solid work in philosophy, history, psychology and sociology faces formidable obstacles

19

in determining what in those disciplines is relevant to problems of the curriculum (and so forth). The professional educator confronted by class after class of students who cannot overcome these obstacles, understandably might do one or two things. He might approach the department of history, philosophy, sociology and psychology with a plea that they design courses that bear more or less directly on his problems or he might try to devise courses of this kind himself. Very often it is the futility of the first approach that makes the second alternative unavoidable.

Broudy reminds us that a professional field of study is distinguished by the way it organizes learning around problems distinctive to the profession:

> In this it differs from an intellectual discipline such as mathematics or physics. Mathematics is constituted of an interrelated set of concepts dealing with quantitative relationships. The professional curriculum of the teaching of mathematics . . . organizes materials in terms of teaching and learning mathematics. Such concerns also distinguish education from law, engineering, medicine and other professions. A distinctive set of problems studied in their foundational and specialist dimensions provides the structural framework for any professional field. (1963, p. 50)

Broudy sets forth a taxonomy in which he proposes four problem areas in education that should be studied: educational aims; the curriculum; school organization, administration, and support; and teaching and learning. The four disciplines that would shed most light on the above problem areas are history, psychology, sociology, and philosophy. It is clear that Broudy's approach, suggested many years ago, influenced NCATE's 1982 and 1995 standards.

Howsam and his colleagues also find fault with the content and teaching of foundations courses. They note that "foundations professors refuse to become involved with field experiences and the problems of practitioners which they perceive as outside the analytic or descriptive function of the discipline" (1976, p. 87). They also argue that "foundations courses are taught as separate disciplines in such a way that students fail to see the interplay between theory and practice" (p. 187). They recommend:

> that a series of changes be made in the formats, conceptual frameworks and delivery modes. . . . To support and strengthen teachers, [they] must become interdisciplinary; unifying in concept and practice; less obscure and more human service functional; problem-based, featuring "theory in practice" modes of inquiry; original and bold in developing explanatory hypotheses; personal and clarifying in terms of beliefs and values; socially activistic and mission centered; and experimental in teaching procedures and delivery modes. (p. 88)

The role of foundations professors is particularly difficult. If they have been prepared well, they are naturally enthusiastic about their respective parent discipline, for example, philosophy. However, many education students do not share that enthusiasm and fail to see how the content relates to the problems of classroom teaching, which they expect their professional courses to cover.

These courses are not designed to solve specific classroom problems. Instead, they are intended to give a context for thinking about problems. As Broudy argues:

> The sociology or even the psychology of education, for example, will not directly help the second-grade teacher to manage her slow learners. . . . Although foundational knowledge does not solve problems, it does prevent our being naive and provincial about them. (1963, p. 53)

Although there is support for including such courses in the preparation curriculum, it is apparent both from practice and from the literature that significant problems persist. Following are some suggestions that may be useful:

1. Identify the concepts, facts, and conditional propositions from the several foundational study areas that would help to illuminate thought and practice in education.
2. Gain consensus from teacher educators and practicing teachers on the appropriateness of teaching these concepts and understandings in the preservice curriculum.

3. Determine when, where, and how the knowledge can best be attained.
4. Ensure that members of the foundations faculty acknowledge and support the above determination.
5. When hiring such professors, ensure that they are committed primarily to the education of teachers.
6. Reward professors who make such commitments and perform their roles well.
7. Ensure that preservice teachers have an adequate general education that will prepare them for all foundational studies.
8. Teach these courses in such a way that students see the interplay between theory and practice.

Pedagogical studies, the second component of professional education, refers to the application of concepts, theories, and research about effective teaching. It also has been called "teaching and learning theory."

Sources of such pedagogical knowledge include teacher professional wisdom gained through classroom experience, knowledge obtained from the social and behavioral sciences (for example, sociology and psychology), knowledge generated within university teacher education units, and knowledge derived from the study of K-12 teaching. Historically, professional wisdom has dominated the content of this curriculum component and frequently has been inseparable from advocacy and commitment (Dunkin and Biddle 1974).

Teacher educators, for the most part former classroom teachers themselves, frequently draw from their personal knowledge and experience. This can be called *craft knowledge*. Curriculum projects on which teacher educators work reflect this propensity. For example, use of professional wisdom dominated decisions about pedagogical curriculum generally, and teaching and learning theory specifically, when teacher educators produced the federally sponsored Comprehensive Elementary Teacher Education Models program (CETEM), an effort to redesign the preservice curriculum for elementary teachers, described in Chapter 2.

Later, efforts to generate competency-based teacher education and so-called generic teaching competencies also relied heavily on craft knowledge, though they also used knowledge from the undergirding disciplines of education (particularly psychology) and knowledge generated from within teacher education units (Bureau of Academic Programs 1978; Dick, Watson, and Kaufman 1981; Dodl et al. 1972).

Professional organizations that influence the teacher education curriculum also tend to be very dependent on use of craft knowledge. For example, the NEA publication, *Excellence in Our Schools* (1982), described in Chapter 2, presents "views of the united teaching profession about needed changes in teacher education." According to NEA, the document "reflects substantial input by NEA members [K-12 teachers] and *represents what practitioners know*" (p. 4).

In addition to craft knowledge, efforts are being made to derive the content of teaching and learning theory courses from knowledge gained through studying teaching and learning in natural classrooms. There is an accumulating body of such *clinical knowledge*. According to Smith:

> There is just as much intellectual challenge in mastering, for example, the concept of "praise," the various ways and conditions of using it, and learning to perform in the classroom according to the rules governing the use of praise as there is in the mastery of a particular concept or principle of philosophy or psychology. (1983, pp. 7-8)

As clinical knowledge increases, it becomes the task of the academic theoretician to provide ways to understand it. For example, why are the effects of praise discrepant? Educational psychologists or philosophers will be held in higher regard if they can, in fact, provide explanations that enable preservice teachers to understand why and how what they do affects classroom outcomes.

The coursework included in this component of teacher education often is referred to as "general and special methods." A general methods course intends to convey what is known about pedagogy, the art and science of teaching, that is of interest and use to all K-12 teachers. Special methods courses, on the other hand, address that which supposedly is different about teaching various grade levels or content specialties, for example, the teaching of art in first grade as opposed to the teaching of physics in senior high.

Teacher education institutions have offered a variety of special methods courses. Elementary teacher education, due to its broad curricular responsibilities, is rife with such courses, labeled "The Teaching of Art," "The Teaching of Health and Physical Education," "Elementary Social Studies Methods," "Reading in the Elementary School," and so on. Like Conant, many academicians and some of the general public believe these courses to be unnecessary, duplicative, and devoid of intellectual content. As a result, this segment of the professional curriculum often is under attack. The defenders, as Gutek points out, "contend that [they] provide the most practical preparation for elementary school teaching" (1970, p. 140).

Conant (1963) viewed the content of general methods classes as basically the same as that taught in courses in general psychology and educational psychology, and he described these methods courses as "unnecessary duplication." His judgment of special methods courses was equally negative. He argued that if particular knowledge or skills are needed, they best can be learned as part of the practicum or student teaching. Conant also eschewed methods courses because there is no agreement on a common body of knowledge that all teachers should have before taking their first full-time job. That may be less the case now than in the past.

In contrast, preservice teachers are in nearly unanimous support of methods courses. Edmundson notes that "It is in the methods courses that students believe that they really begin to learn how to be teachers" (1990, p. 720). Furthermore, she reports:

> Students and faculty members who responded to the SEE survey saw methods courses as potentially more important to students' future success as teachers than either educational psychology courses or foundations courses. But both groups

24

rated methods courses lower than early field experience or student teaching. (p. 720)

What exactly should preservice teachers know about teaching? Goodlad notes in "A Study of Schooling" (1983) that:

> At all levels of schooling, a very few teaching procedures — explaining or lecturing, monitoring seatwork, and quizzing — accounted for most of those we observed overall in our sample of 1,016 classrooms. Teachers varied in the quality of their lecturing, for example, but "teacher talk" was by far the dominant classroom activity. (p. 552)

If this is the case, then teacher education has the responsibility to ensure that teachers at least do these things well, that is, explaining, lecturing, monitoring, quizzing. It would seem appropriate that gaining competence in these skills should be part of pedagogical study. The National Education Association long has argued that preservice teachers should be taught so that they can "start their careers with a background of experiences that allows them to handle classroom situations comfortably" (1982, p. 7).

According to the NEA report, *Excellence in Our Schools*, teachers must be prepared to perform three critical functions: 1) facilitating learning and knowing the unique characteristics of students; 2) managing the classroom, or organizing the classroom to stimulate learning and foster discipline; and 3) making professional decisions, such as deciding what to teach.

Smith et al. (1969) argue that:

> Teachers fail because they have not been trained calmly to analyze [classroom and school] situations against a firm background of relevant theory. . . . If the teacher is incapable of understanding classroom situations, the actions he takes will often increase his difficulties. (pp. 28-29)

If this assertion is correct, then it is incumbent upon those preparing teachers to provide them with opportunities to reflect on significant teaching situations and problems and to help them to draw on related theory to analyze and understand the situations or resolve the problems (Cruickshank et al. 1980).

Two publications from the American Association of Colleges for Teacher Education suggest curricula for pedagogical studies. The first (Howsam et al. 1976) calls for teacher acquisition of "a broad repertoire of classroom behaviors and skills, grounded in professional and academic knowledge" (p. 88). Howsam and his colleagues describe behaviors and skills that are similar to a set of 33 used in the preservice curriculum at the University of Houston. They organize these skills in 11 categories:

1. Diagnosis and evaluation,
2. Organizing the classroom,
3. Goals and objectives,
4. Planning,
5. Communicating,
6. Instructing,
7. Managing,
8. Interpersonal relations,
9. Evaluation,
10. Self-improvement, and
11. Colleagues and other professionals (pp. 160- 161).

The second publication from the American Association of Colleges for Teacher Education (Scannell et al. 1983) describes both requisite generic teaching knowledge and skills and specialized pedagogical knowledge and skills. The generic teaching knowledge and skills are arranged under eight teacher functions:

1. Analyzing and interpreting student abilities,
2. Designing instruction to meet learner needs,
3. Conducting instruction,
4. Managing the classroom,
5. Managing student conduct,
6. Promoting classroom communication,
7. Evaluating learning, and
8. Arranging for conferral and referral opportunities.

One of the most intensive efforts to incorporate pedagogical theory into the preservice curriculum was undertaken more than

30 years ago by the Teacher Education and Media (TEAM) project (LaGrone 1964). This project outlined five courses related to teaching and learning theory. Three seem to fit the definition of teaching theory: "The Analytic Study of Teaching," "Design for Teaching-Learning," and "Evaluation of Teaching Competencies." These courses and related others are described briefly in Chapter 2.

In addition to research about how teachers teach, the pedagogical studies component of professional education also should include the research on how students learn. Unfortunately, persons preparing to teach often are given the most minimal exposure to what is known about learning. Their knowledge usually is limited to what is contained in a chapter in a psychology or educational psychology text.

The following suggestions are offered to improve the pedagogical component of the preservice curriculum:

1. Agreement must be reached on the content of these courses.
2. The content for these courses should be selected, to the extent possible, from empirically verified findings about teaching and learning, rather than based on personal opinions or biases.
3. Greater attention should be given to having teachers learn skills for solving classroom problems.
4. Sustained efforts should be undertaken to collect and codify teaching and learning theory. The result could be a manual that provides concise but authoritative information for teacher educators (and practicing teachers). Such a manual might be similar to the desk references used by physicians and veterinarians.
5. Whether knowledge of learning theory is gained in educational psychology or in some other course, it must be a highly visible component in the preservice professional curriculum.
6. Those who teach special methods courses in their subject areas should keep in mind the differences between general

and special methods. Special methods courses are designed to ensure that preservice teachers know the particular K-12 curriculum they will teach and the special approaches or alternative ways of coming to understand it. They should not replicate what preservice teachers have learned in other courses.

7. Those who teach methods course are the glue that holds the professional program together. These persons, above all others, need a broad understanding of the whole preservice curriculum and the role that teaching and learning theory plays therein.

Integrative Studies

NCATE (1995) labels the fourth component of the preservice teacher preparation curriculum as *integrative studies*. However, it is more commonly known as on- and off-campus laboratory and clinical experiences. The purpose of these experiences — sometimes real and sometimes contrived or simulated — is to provide preservice teachers with settings in which they may study teaching and practice what they have learned in general, content, and professional education.

Off-campus, field, or school-based experiences include: *observation*, where preservice teachers observe in K-12 classrooms but do not engage in teaching; part-time *participation*, where engagement in real teaching is limited to trying out selected teaching abilities (for example, leading a small-group discussion) following procedures learned in methods classes; part-time *apprenticeships*, where preservice teachers learn by practical experience under the guidance of skilled teachers; and finally full-time *practicum* or student teaching, where preservice teachers work in a classroom for an extended period of time and are expected to assume most, if not all, responsibility for teaching.

The contrived or simulated teaching experiences usually are undertaken on campus. They include: *peer teaching*; *mirror teaching*, which merely is videotaped peer teaching; and *microteach-*

ing, which is a form of peer teaching whereby one preservice teacher teaches a small group of peers with the major purpose of practicing one or more technical skills, such as the ability to use "probing questions." Other experiences of the contrived type are *simulations*, where, for example, preservice teachers assume the role of a teacher in a fictitious classroom in order to resolve commonly reported teaching problems, and *Reflective Teaching*, where preservice teachers teach brief lessons to peers, are given feedback by peers regarding their success in presenting the lessons, and then reflect on the teaching they have done and what they have learned about teaching and learning (Cruickshank 1991). Still another type of simulated experience is the use of *protocol materials*, where, for example, preservice teachers view a videotape of a significant event in a classroom and then are provided with related theoretical knowledge that illuminates the event. Several forms of on-campus laboratory and clinical experiences are described more fully in Chapter 3.

Thus preservice teachers can have direct experience with reality in regular classrooms, and they also can have direct experiences with *models of reality* in contrived, simulated settings. Both types of experiences can be categorized as laboratory or clinical. Lindsey describes a *laboratory experience* as:

> a place for the systematic study of teaching — a place where a student may discover what teaching IS and how the many and diverse variables in a complex teaching-learning environment interact with each other. It is a place where a prospective teacher may test his knowledge about teaching and verify or modify his understanding of that knowledge. (1971, p. 84)

Using Lindsey's definition, all school-based and on-campus teaching activities potentially qualify as laboratory experiences. However, in practice, many fall short. Student teaching is a good example. While it has the necessary conditions to become a laboratory activity, it frequently is not, because student teachers are not truly viewed and treated as students of teaching involved in discovering, testing, reflecting, modifying, and so forth. Rather, too often student teaching is best characterized as learning to cook in someone else's kitchen, or modeling the "master."

Clinical experience is the term reserved for situations in which preservice teachers actually analyze and treat learners in a manner similar to that of physicians who diagnose and prescribe to patients. To be considered a clinical experience in preservice teaching, Mills requires that, among other things, the activity must: present a case or problem — either simulated or real — that relates directly to school-aged children and youth; provide opportunity for the preservice teacher to study and practice analytic, diagnostic, and prescriptive skills; and provide systematic feedback to assist the preservice teacher in developing and improving performance (n.d., p. 9).

Laboratory, clinical, and practicum experiences have been included in the teacher preparation curriculum since at least the early 19th century. They have been supported strongly by the Commission on Teacher Education (1946) and by Conant (1963), who describes laboratory experiences positively:

> It seems clear that the future . . . teacher has much to learn that can be learned only in the . . . classroom. . . . I would argue that all education courses for elementary teachers . . . be accompanied by "laboratory experiences" providing for the observation and teaching of children. To some extent limited use of film and television can take the place of direct classroom observation. (p. 161)

Students see student teaching as the part of their program that has the greatest potential for contributing to their future success as teachers. They also see it as the most interesting part and as the part that pays the most attention to their individual needs. In the Study of the Education of Educators, student teaching was rated highest in influencing educational values and beliefs, with the influence of cooperating teachers rated a close second (Edmundson 1990, p. 720).

The NCATE *Standards* (1995) note that field experiences provide teacher candidates with opportunities to:

relate principles and theories from the conceptual framework(s) to actual practice in classrooms and schools; create meaningful learning experiences for all students; study and practice in a variety of communities, with students of different ages, and with culturally diverse and exceptional populations. Field experiences [should] encourage reflection by candidates and include feedback from higher education faculty, school faculty, and peers; . . . should be a minimum of ten weeks of full-time student teaching, or its equivalent. (p. 7)

Among the most important issues associated with laboratory and clinical experiences is how they should be sequenced and how one relates to the other. According to Nolan:

Our failure to be cognizant of the distinction in terminology between early professional laboratory experiences and practicum experiences . . . has resulted in a professional viewpoint which sees the purpose of student teaching as the development of teaching skills which were practiced previously in earlier field experiences . . . [whereas] the purpose of student teaching (is) a continuation of the scientific inquiry, hypothesis testing and experimentation which were first practiced in the relatively safe environment of early laboratory experiences. (1983, p. 52)

Nolan argues that certain on-campus laboratory experiences should occur before student teaching, and that "they should be designed to foster *reflective criticism* of the methods of instruction and the purposes of education and enable the preservice teacher to be a more thoughtful and alert student of teaching" (1983, p. 49). Therefore, "the apprenticeship" should occur only after the preservice teacher has developed the methods of reflective inquiry. He notes that more on-campus laboratory experiences, such as reflective teaching, simulations, or protocol materials, are a necessary but missing link between classroom theory and the practicum.

A related problem associated with laboratory, clinical, and practicum experiences is the failure to make these experiences laboratory-like. Lindsey's (1971) definition of laboratory experiences contains such explicit requirements as the "systematic study of teaching," "discovery of how the many and diverse variables in a complex teaching-learning environment interact," "testing and verifying knowledge of teaching," and so forth. It also demands practice *with feedback*.

Howsam et al. (1976) describe the ideal laboratory experiences in teacher education:

> The teacher education classroom should be a laboratory for the study and development of teaching knowledge and skills. This laboratory should be expanded to include instructional procedures such as microteaching, simulation, modeling and demonstration. These procedures help students to confront a controlled reality by concentrating on particular teaching-learning behaviors until they attain adequate levels of skills and confidence. When students do encounter the complexity of a regular classroom, they will have experienced a planned series of teaching acts in a minimally threatening environment, with immediate feedback and experienced supervision. (p. 93)

Unfortunately, in practice, laboratory teaching experiences fall short of the ideal. A problem associated with clinical experience is the failure to provide such opportunities. There have been few opportunities for the preservice teacher in the field or on campus to engage in diagnostic and prescriptive activities and subsequently to receive systematic feedback, which are the essences of the clinical approach. Furthermore, teacher educators have tended to rely on craft knowledge or the application of knowledge from psychology and sociology. Smith (1983) contends that reliance on use of academic knowledge in clinical situations is inadequate, because we cannot deduce effective teaching from what is gleaned from another discipline. Rather, he argues that we must study effective teaching in its own right in order to discover professional content that can be applied to clinical experience. The more we study teaching and learning *in the classroom*, the more we will accumulate knowledge that has a direct relationship to teaching practice.

Another issue is who controls field experiences. The primary responsibility has tended to rest with the teacher education units in colleges and universities that have been state approved to offer teacher preparation programs. However, local school districts also have vested interests, because they provide the workplace. The issue of control arises at many points, including when the workplace is selected, when cooperating or mentor teachers are chosen, when the roles of the preservice teacher and mentor are defined, when conferencing is done, and when preservice teachers are evaluated.

A major goal associated with the practicum experience is enhancing its image among teacher educators and academicians. As long as it continues to be viewed as simply an apprenticeship, it will be shunned by those who view their professional role as more important than just monitoring behavior. As the practicum experience becomes more laboratory and clinically oriented, its image surely will improve.

A further problem associated with practicum experiences has been the failure to integrate knowledge derived from studies of teaching and school effectiveness. As the results of such research accumulate and are validated, it is incumbent on practicum supervisors to ensure that preservice teachers not only know but can apply what is known about, for example, "clarity," "time on task," "with-it-ness," and so forth.

McIntyre (1983) describes some of the other continuing issues associated with field experiences: What should be learned from field experiences? How valid are current types of field experiences? What effects do they have? What are the roles and relationships of preservice teachers, cooperating teachers, and university supervisors? How can persons be better prepared for these roles? How should field experiences be structured? How can field experiences be made more like laboratory experiences in order to foster inquiry and reflection, rather than being merely an apprenticeship experience? How should preservice teacher performance in the field be evaluated?

Some suggestions for improving the laboratory, clinical, and practicum component of the preservice curriculum include:

1. Obtain consensus regarding the outcomes of these experiences.
2. Determine to what extent the various experiences are valid for each outcome.
3. Gain consensus on the roles and relationships of persons involved in the experiences.
4. Determine how best to prepare each subgroup for its role.
5. Gain consensus on how the variety of experiences should be structured and when they should be presented.
6. Reach agreement on how preservice teachers should be evaluated during these experiences.
7. Support the identification and verification of knowledge that can be used to enhance such experiences.

Guidelines for Improving the Curriculum

Here are some broad guidelines that, if implemented, should lead to improvements in both the curriculum and how it is delivered. These guidelines are offered in addition to the more specific suggestions made throughout this chapter.

1. The nature of the curriculum and its effect should be assessed regularly by persons representing general studies, content studies, professional and pedagogical studies, and integrative studies. This would include K-12 teachers. An individual from the professional education unit should be responsible for this review function.
2. The preparation curriculum should derive from a conceptualization of what it is like, or should be like, to be a teacher. Emphasis should be on what teachers need to know and to be able to do.
3. The preparation curriculum should reflect the best thinking and research related to teacher preparation. Some of this best thinking is contained in reform proposals described in Chapter 2.

4. All those who are involved in teacher preparation or planning to become so should understand the total curriculum and what their role is in its promotion and success. This includes the faculty who teach general and content studies.
5. Faculty involved in teacher preparation should themselves be generally well-educated and have strong subject matter knowledge and teaching ability.
6. Preservice teachers should be reminded of the total scope of their curriculum and how each subcomponent and class or activity contributes to their preparation.
7. Faculty and graduate students should be encouraged to conduct inquiry related to the preparation curriculum.
8. A permanent teacher education curriculum council should be formed at the national level to promote improved preparation curricula. The council would represent all stakeholders in teacher preparation but would be mostly the responsibility of the chief state school officers, because education and teacher education are state duties.

References

Adler, M. *The Paideia Proposal: An Educational Manifesto.* New York: Macmillan, 1982.

American Association of Colleges for Teacher Education (AACTE). *Task Force on Extended Programs Report.* Washington, D.C., 1982.

American Association of Colleges for Teacher Education (AACTE). *A Call for Change in Teacher Education.* Washington, D.C., 1985.

American Association of Colleges for Teacher Education (AACTE). *RATE V: Teaching Teachers. Facts & Figures.* Washington, D.C., 1991.

American Association of Colleges for Teacher Education (AACTE). *Alternative Paths to Teaching: A Directory of Postbaccalaureate Programs.* Washington, D.C., 1993.

Armstrong, W.E. "The Teacher Education Curricula." *Journal of Teacher Education* 8 (1957): 1-16.

Borman, K.M. "Foundations of Education in Teacher Education." In *Handbook of Research on Teacher Education*, edited by W.R. Houston, M. Haberman, and J. Sikula. New York, Macmillan, 1990.

Broudy, H.S. *The Scholars and the Public Schools.* Columbus: Ohio State University Press, 1963.

Broudy, H.S. *The Real World of the Public School.* New York: Harcourt Brace Jovanovich, 1972.

Bureau of Academic Programs. *More from Performance and Competency Based Teacher Education Inventories of Specialized Competencies.* Harrisburg: Pennsylvania Department of Education, Office of Higher Education, 1978.

Carnegie Forum on Education and the Economy, Task Force on Teaching as a Profession. *A Nation Prepared: Teacher's for the 21st Century.* Washington, D.C., 1986.

Chandler, B.J.; Powell, D.; and Hazzard, W. *Education and the New Teacher.* New York: Dodd, Mead, 1971.

Commission on Teacher Education. *The Improvement of Teacher Education: A Final Report by the Commission on Teacher Education.* Washington, D.C.: American Council on Education, 1946.

Conant, J. *The Education of American Teachers.* New York: McGraw-Hill, 1963.

Council of Learned Societies in Education. *Standards for Academic and Professional Instruction in Foundations of Education, Educational Studies and Educational Policy Studies.* Ann Arbor, Mich.: Prakken, 1986.

Cruickshank, D.R. *Reflective Teaching.* Rev. ed. Bloomington, Ind.: Phi Delta Kappa, 1991.

Cruickshank, D.R.; Applegate, J.; Holton, J.; Mager, J.; Myers, B.; Novak, C.; and Tracey, K. *Teaching Is Tough.* Englewood Cliffs, N.J.: Prentice-Hall, 1980.

Dick, W.; Watson, K.; and Kaufman, R. "Deriving Competencies: Consensus Versus Model Building." *Educational Research* 10, no. 8 (1981): 5-10.

Dodl, N.; Elfner, E.; Becker, J.; Halstead, J.; Jung, H.; Nelson, P.; Purinton, S.; and Wegele, P. *Florida Catalog of Teacher Competencies.* Tallahassee: Florida State University, 1972.

Dunkin, M., and Biddle, B. *The Study of Teaching.* New York: Holt, Rinehart and Winston, 1974.

Edmundson, P.J. "A Normative Look at the Curriculum in Teacher Education." *Phi Delta Kappan* 71 (May 1990): 717-22.

Feiman-Nemser, S. "Teacher Preparation: Structural and Conceptual Alternatives." In *Handbook of Research on Teacher Education*, edited by W.R. Houston, M. Haberman, and J. Sikula. New York: Macmillan, 1990.

Florida Department of Education. *Florida Teacher Certification Examination.* Tallahassee: State of Florida Department of Education on Teacher Certification Section, 1982.

Galambos, E.C. *Teacher Preparation: The Anatomy of a College Degree.* Atlanta: Southern Regional Education Board; Washington, D.C.: National Endowment for the Humanities, 1985. ERIC Document Reproduction Service No. ED 258 957.

Goodlad, J.I. "A Study of Schooling: Some Implications for School Improvement." *Phi Delta Kappan* 64 (April 1983): 552-58.

Goodlad, J.I. *Teachers for Our Nation's Schools.* San Francisco: Jossey-Bass, 1990.

Gutek, G.L. *An Historical Introduction to American Education.* New York: Harper & Row, 1970.

Harvard Committee on General Education. *General Education in a Free Society.* Cambridge, Mass., 1945.

"Help! Teachers Can't Teach!" *Time,* 16 June 1980, pp. 54-63.

Holmes Group. *Tomorrow's Teachers.* East Lansing, Mich., 1986.

Howsam, R.B.; Corrigan, D; Denemark, G.; and Nash, R. *Educating a Profession.* Washington, D.C.: American Association of Colleges for Teacher Education, 1976.

Koerner, J. *The Miseducation of American Teachers.* Boston: Houghton Mifflin, 1963.

LaGrone, H. *A Proposal for the Revision of the Pre-service Professional Component of a Program of Teacher Education.* Washington, D.C.: American Association of Colleges for Teacher Education, 1964.

Lindsey, M. "Teachers, Education of: Laboratory Experiences." In *The Encyclopedia of Education.* New York: Macmillan, Free Press, 1971.

McIntyre, D.J. *Field Experiences in Teacher Education.* Washington, D.C.: Foundation for Excellence in Teacher Education, ERIC Clearinghouse of Teacher Education, 1983.

Mills, P. "Integrating Clinical Experiences Within the Teacher Education Curriculum at Bowling Green State University." In *Clinical Experience in Teacher Education,* edited by J. Gress. Columbus: Ohio Association of Teacher Educators and Ohio Association of Colleges for Teacher Education, n.d.

National Association of State Directors of Teacher Education and Certification (NASDTEC). *Standards for State Approval of Teacher Education, 1989 Revised Edition.* Salt Lake City: Utah State Office of Education, Curriculum Principles and Patterns Section, 1989.

National Council for Accreditation of Teacher Education (NCATE). *Standards for the Accreditation of Teacher Education.* Washington, D.C., 1982.

National Council for Accreditation of Teacher Education (NCATE). *Standards, Procedures, and Policies for the Accreditation of Professional Education Units.* Washington, D.C., 1995.

National Education Association. *Excellence in Our Schools: Teacher Education, an Action Plan.* Washington, D.C., 1982.

Nolan, J.F. "Professional Laboratory Experiences: The Missing Link in Teacher Education." *Journal of Teacher Education* 33, no. 4 (1983): 49-53.

Parker, F. "Reforming U.S. Teacher Education in the 1990s." 1993. ERIC Document Reproduction Services No. ED 358 084.

Ritsch, F.F. "Teacher Preparation and the Liberal Arts." *Educational Forum* 45 (1981): 405-10.

Scannell, D.P.; Corrigan, D.C.; Denemark, G.; Dieterle, L.; Egbert, R.; and Nielsen, R. *Educating a Profession: Profile of a Beginning Teacher.* Washington, D.C.: American Association of Colleges for Teacher Education, 1983.

Schein, E.H. *Professional Education.* New York: McGraw-Hill, 1972.

Sewall, G.T. "Against Anomie and Amnesia: What Basic Education Means in the Eighties." *Phi Delta Kappan* 63 (May 1982): 603-606.

Sherwin, S. *Teacher Education: A Status Report.* Princeton, N.J.: Educational Testing Service, 1974.

Silberman, C.E. *Crisis in the Classroom. The Remaking of American Education.* New York: Random House, 1970.

Smith, B.O. *Design for a School of Pedagogy.* Washington, D.C.: U.S. Government Printing Office, 1980.

Smith, B.O. "Teacher Education in Transition." Paper presented at the annual meeting of the American Association of Colleges for Teacher Education, Detroit, February 1983.

Smith, B.O.; Cohen, S.B.; and Pearl, A. *Teachers for the Real World.* Washington, D.C.: American Association of Colleges for Teacher Education, 1969.

Stengel, R. "Quality, Not Just Quantity: The Paideia Proposal Aims to Reform America's Schools." *Time,* 6 September 1982, p. 59.

Ward, C. "Teacher Education Admissions Testing." *American Association of Colleges for Teacher Education Briefs* 9 (1981): 4-5.

Whitehead, A.N. *The Aims of Education.* New York: Mentor Books, 1949.

Wilson, K.G., and Davis, B. *Redesigning Education*. New York: Henry Holt, 1994.

Wisniewski, R. "Linking Teacher Education and Liberal Learning." In *Integrating Liberal Learning and Professional Education*, edited by R.A. Armour and B.S. Fuhrmann. New Directions for Teaching and Learning No. 40. San Francisco: Jossey-Bass, 1989.

Wong, M.J., and Osguthorpe, R.T. "The Continuing Domination of the Four-Year Teacher Education Program: A National Survey." *Journal of Teacher Education* 44, no. 1 (1993): 64-70.

Related Readings

American Association of Colleges for Teacher Education. *Guidelines for the Preparation of Elementary School Teachers*. Washington, D.C., 1988.

Baratz-Snowdon, J. "National Board for Professional Teaching Standards: Update." *ERIC Digest* (1992). ERIC Document Reproduction Services No. ED 351 336.

Bartos, R., and Souter, F. "What Are We Teaching in Educational Foundations?" *Journal of Teacher Education* 33, no. 2 (1982): 45-47.

Bennett, S.M. "Recent Research on Teaching: A Dream, a Belief, and a Model." *British Journal of Educational Psychology* 48 (1978): 127-47.

Bloom, B.S. *Human Characteristics and School Learning*. New York: McGraw-Hill, 1976.

Borrowman, M.L., ed. *Teacher Education in America*. New York: Teachers College Press, 1966.

Boyer, E.L., and Levine, A. *A Quest for Common Learning: The Aims of General Education*. Washington, D.C.: Carnegie Foundation for the Advancement of Teaching, 1981.

Brophy, J., and Good, T. "Teacher Behavior and Student Achievement." In *Handbook of Research on Teaching*, 3rd ed., edited by M.C. Wittrock. New York: Macmillan, 1986.

Bruner, J.S. *Toward a Theory of Instruction*. New York: Norton, 1966.

Carter, K. "Teachers' Knowledge and Learning to Teach." In *Handbook of Research on Teacher Education*, edited by W.R. Houston, M. Haberman, and J. Sikula. New York: Macmillan, 1990.

Clark, M.C.; Snow, R.; and Shavelson, R. "Three Experiments on Learning to Teach." *Journal of Teacher Education* 27, no. 2 (1976): 174-79.

Cogan, M.L. "The Academic Major in the Education of Teachers." In *Improving Teacher Education in the United States,* edited by Stanley Elam. Bloomington, Ind.: Phi Delta Kappa, 1967.

Commission on Teacher Education. *The Improvement of Teacher Education: A Final Report by the Commission on Teacher Education.* Washington, D.C.: American Council on Education, 1946.

Cottrell, D.P., ed. *Teacher Education for a Free People.* Washington, D.C.: American Association of Colleges for Teacher Education, 1956.

Cruickshank, D.R. *Blueprints for Teacher Education: A Review of Phase II Proposals for the USDE Comprehensive Elementary Teacher Education (CETEM) Program.* Washington, D.C.: U.S. Department of Health, Education and Welfare, 1970.

Cruickshank, D.R. "Conceptualizing a Process for Teacher Education Curriculum Development." *Journal of Teacher Education* 11, no. 1 (1972): 73-82.

Cruickshank, D.R. "Toward a Model to Guide Inquiry in Teacher Education." *Journal of Teacher Education* 35, no. 6 (1984): 43-48.

Cruickshank, D.R. *Research that Informs Teachers and Teacher Educators.* Bloomington, Ind.: Phi Delta Kappa Educational Foundation, 1990.

Cruickshank, D.R., and Armaline, W.D. "Field Experiences in Teacher Education: Considerations and Recommendations." *Journal of Teacher Education* 37, no. 3 (1986): 34-40.

Cruickshank, D.R.; Bainer, D.L.; and Metcalf, K.K. *The Act of Teaching.* New York: McGraw-Hill, 1995.

Dewey, J. *Democracy and Education.* New York: Macmillan, 1916.

Dewey, J. "The Relationship of Theory to Practice in Education." In *Teacher Education in America: A Documentary History*, edited by M.L. Borrowman. New York: Teachers College Press, 1965.

Ferguson, P., and Womack, S.T. "The Impact of Subject Matter and Education Coursework on Teaching Performance." *Journal of Teacher Education* 44, no. 1 (1993): 55-63.

Flanders, N.A. *Analyzing Teacher Behavior.* Reading, Mass.: Addison-Wesley, 1970.

Florida Beginning Teacher Program. *Handbook of the Florida Performance Measurement System.* Tallahassee: Florida Office of Teacher Education, Certification and Inservice Staff Development, 1983.

Glaser, R. "Components of a Psychology of Instruction: Toward a Science of Design." *Review of Educational Research* 46 (1976): 1-24.

Good, T., and McCaslin, M. "Teaching Effectiveness." In *The Encyclopedia of Education,* 6th ed., edited by M. Alkin. New York: Macmillan, 1992.

Haertel, G.D.; Walberg, H.J.; and Weinstein, T. "Psychological Models of Educational Performance: A Theoretical Synthesis of Constructs." *Review of Educational Research* 53 (1983): 75-91.

Hamilton, R., and Ghatala, E. *Learning and Instruction.* New York: McGraw-Hill, 1994.

Harnischfeger, A., and Wiley, D. "The Teaching-Learning Process in Elementary Schools: A Synoptic View." *Curriculum Inquiry* 6 (1976): 5-43.

Houston, W.R.; Haberman, M.; and Sikula, J., eds. *Handbook of Research on Teacher Education.* New York: Macmillan, 1990.

Howsam, R.B. "The Workplace: Does It Hamper Professionalization of Pedagogy?" *Phi Delta Kappan* 62 (October 1980): 93-96.

Joyce, B., and Weil, M. *Models of Teaching.* Englewood Cliffs, N.J.: Prentice-Hall, 1986.

Kennedy, M.M. "Some Surprising Findings in How Teachers Learn to Teach." *Educational Leadership* 49, no. 3 (1991): 14-17.

Loewenberg-Ball, D.L., and McDiarmid, G.W. "The Subject Matter Preparation of Teachers." In *Handbook of Research on Teacher Education,* edited by W.R. Houston, M. Haberman, and J. Sikula. New York: Macmillan, 1990.

National Society for the Study of Education. *The Psychology of Teaching Methods.* Chicago: University of Chicago Press, 1976.

Ornstein, A.C. "The Trend Toward Increased Professionalism for Teachers." *Phi Delta Kappan* 63 (November 1981): 196-98.

Phenix, P.H. *Realms of Meaning: A Philosophy of the Curriculum for General Education.* New York: McGraw-Hill, 1964.

Philosophy of Education Society. "Standards for Academic and Professional Instruction in Philosophy of Education." *Educational Theory* 30 (1980): 265-68.

Seaborg, G.T., and Bazun, J. *The Sciences and the Humanities in the Schools After a Decade of Reform.* Washington, D.C.: Council for Basic Education, 1966.

Smith, B.O. "The Liberal Arts and Teacher Education." In *The Liberal Arts and Teacher Education,* edited by D. Bigelow. Lincoln: University of Nebraska Press, 1971.

Smith, B.O. *On the Content of Teacher Education.* Tampa: University of South Florida, n.d.

Taylor, H. "Philosophy and Education." In *Five Fields and Teacher Education,* edited by D.B. Gowin and C. Richardson. Ithaca, N.Y.: Cornell University, 1965.

Tom, A. *The Case for Maintaining Teacher Education at the Undergraduate Level.* St. Louis: Washington University, Coalition of Teacher Education Programs, 1986. ERIC Document Reproduction Service No. ED 267 067.

Weaver, W.T. "In Search of Quality: The Need for Talent in Teaching." *Phi Delta Kappan* 61 (September 1979): 29-32, 46.

Winter, D.G.; McClelland, D.C.; and Steward, A.J. *A New Case for the Liberal Arts.* San Francisco: Jossey-Bass, 1981.

Chapter 2
REFORMING TEACHER EDUCATION: SUMMARIES OF 29 PROPOSALS

Following World War II, and particularly since the 1960s, a flood of different ideas for teacher preparation have emerged from a variety of sources, including the federal government, private foundations, teacher associations, university teacher education units, and interested individuals. In many cases these proposed reforms were intended to overcome the perceived failure of the existing teacher preparation curricula to meet the scientific, economic, and social demands placed on schools.

Following is a review of some prominent reform proposals made over the past four decades. This list of proposals is not complete; rather, it consists of those that seem most interesting and worthwhile. The proposals are presented roughly in the chronological order of their publication or appearance, though many overlap in time.

1. A Harvard President's Curriculum

Former Harvard President James Conant brought the problems of teacher education to the attention of the public when his book, *The Education of American Teachers,* reached the best-seller list. Based on a two-year study that took Conant and his staff to 77 colleges and state education offices, the book offered numerous recommendations to state boards of education, state legislatures, local school boards, teacher education institutions, and voluntary accrediting agencies.

In general, Conant suggests that each college or university preparing teachers be permitted to develop whatever program of teacher education it considers best, subject to two conditions. First, the institution's president, on behalf of the entire faculty, must certify that the candidate is adequately prepared to teach at a specific level or in specific fields. Second, the institution, in conjunction with a public school, must establish a state-approved student-teaching program.

Having said that, Conant gives considerable attention to the general studies, content studies, and professional education requirements for a bachelor's degree. For general education, he advises that half the students' time for four years be devoted to "broad *academic* education." This would include the continued study of subjects begun in secondary schools: literature, history, government, mathematics, natural sciences, geography, art, and music. Those disciplines should be studied until the prospective teacher "has attained enough competence to teach the subject to a 12th-grade average class" (p. 94). He adds courses in foreign language, English ("the nature of the language"), philosophy, sociology, anthropology, economics, political science, and psychology, the last six subjects to be taught at an introductory level. Chapter 5 of his book describes a 20-course, 60-semester-hour academic program. Clearly, Conant expects teachers to be generally well-educated, but he also expects such education to begin during their secondary school years.

Conant argues that:

> Only through pursuing a subject well beyond the introductory level can the student gain a coherent picture of the subject, get a glimpse of the vast reaches of knowledge, feel the cutting edge of disciplined training, and discover the satisfactions of a scholarly habit of mind. (p. 106)

Thus he proposes that prospective English, biology, or mathematics teachers complete a concentration of at least 12 courses, or somewhat more that a full year of college, in their subject specialty.

Conant then proposes a curriculum of 30 semester hours of coursework in professional education. He arranges this professional coursework in four broad components, plus student teaching. He calls the first component the democratic social component. The purpose of that component is to prepare teachers to develop the proper attitudes in pupils, for example, "future citizens whose actions will assure the survival of our *free* society" (p. 114). The second component would focus on social behavior, specifically on how social behavior emerges in groups of children. It would address such critical questions as "What kind of social behavior do we want to develop?" The third component focuses on child development more generally. Finally, preservice teachers would study principles of teaching. This last component would focus on helping preservice teachers to learn to do "what good schoolteachers do." These mostly pedagogical tasks include: selecting and organizing instructional materials, presenting information in a form understandable by the young, working with diverse pupils, maintaining discipline, developing interests in fields of study, reporting to parents and the community, and justifying or changing the school's efforts and curriculum.

More specifically, elementary preservice teachers would take courses on child growth and development; a course in history, philosophy, or sociology of education; courses in teaching reading; workshops on the content and methods of elementary school subjects; and year-long laboratory experiences and student teaching. For secondary preservice teachers, he advocates educational psychology; philosophy, history, or sociology of education; special methods of teaching; and practice teaching.

According to Conant, "the one indisputably essential element in professional education is student teaching" (p. 142). All the rest, he says, should be determined by the entire college or university faculty.

Conant's position demands a strong general education component, a guarantee that teachers would thoroughly know the subjects they are to teach, and vastly improved student teaching. He is ambivalent about pedagogy, at one place denying its value and at another providing specific suggestions for its improvement.

2. The TEAM Project

In 1964 and 1967, the American Association of Colleges for Teacher Education (AACTE) published two related documents with implications for the preservice teacher education curriculum. Both resulted from a 27-month, federally sponsored effort, titled "A Project to Improve the Professional Sequence in Preservice Teacher Education Through the Selective and Planned Use of New Media." The project became better known as the TEAM Project (Teacher Education and Media).

The first document, referred to as the LaGrone report (1964), was an effort to present an outline for preservice professional content. After analyzing the factors related to "learning, structure, and media," project director Herbert LaGrone recommended five preservice courses that have content of common value to all teachers. These courses are:

1. *The Analytic Study of Teaching*. The topics included in this course would be: developing a concept of teaching; knowing and being able to use paradigms, models, or schema of teaching; knowing and being able to use four methods to analyze verbal discourse within the classroom; knowing and being able to analyze nonverbal communication in the classroom; assessing the social-emotional climate in the classroom; studying the classroom group as a social system; and gaining knowledge of the nature of leadership style.

2. *Structure and Uses of Knowledge*. This course gives attention to typical uses of knowledge, selecting and using content, and understanding how content can be learned and taught.

3. *Concepts of Human Development and Learning*. The topics for this course include the structure of intellect, cognitive growth, concept formation, cognitive learning styles, inquiry training, readiness and motivation, and evaluation of learning.

4. *Designs for Teaching-Learning*. This course integrates and applies the information obtained in the first three courses. It gives attention to teaching strategies, designing learning units, teaching objectives, instructional systems, and programmed instruction.

5. *Demonstration and Evaluation of Teaching Competencies.* This final course in the series focuses on the teacher behaviors related to teaching and learning and practicing and demonstrating these teacher behaviors in planned trial experiences. It also centers on solving classroom problems and on theories of instruction.

The second TEAM document, *Conceptual Models in Teacher Education* (Verduin 1967), contains presentations by then-leading education researchers and theoreticians whose work influenced the first TEAM document. Accordingly, this second document elaborates on the suggestions for the five courses advocated by the first document.

Overall, the TEAM project garnered some of the best thinking of that time concerning preservice teacher education. Unfortunately, some of the ideas were presented in a technical manner and, perhaps, were too difficult for many practitioners to decipher easily.

3. Teacher Corps

The Teacher Corps was funded under Title V of the Higher Education Act of 1965 (P.L. 89-329) primarily to improve the quality of teachers for schools in low-income urban and rural areas. President Lyndon Johnson, on a surprise visit to the National Education Association's annual convention in Atlantic City on 2 July 1965, announced its inception, noting that the Teacher Corps would:

> enlist thousands of dedicated teachers to work alongside of local teachers in the city slums and in areas of local poverty. . . . They will be young people, preparing for teaching careers. They [also] will be experienced teachers, willing to give a year to the places in their country that need them the most. (National Advisory Council 1975, p. 1)

Since the Teacher Corps was an instrument of federal policy, it was politically sensitive and subject to considerable swings in its recruitment policies and educational programs. With the unexpected surplus of teachers in the early 1970s, the Teacher Corps shifted its training emphasis from "young people preparing for teaching careers" to professional development or retraining practicing teachers.

Over the years, the Teacher Corps advocated a number of changes in preservice teacher education. Many of these emphases were developed as part of other federally sponsored teacher education projects, but they were mandated to be implemented by Teacher Corps projects. The emphases included teaching the disadvantaged (both low-income and learning disabled), recruiting minority persons into teaching, competency-based teacher education, and the use of *portal schools*, where teachers could be inducted gradually into classrooms.

As a consequence of Teacher Corps recruitment and training, Teacher Corps graduates were reported to be more effective:

> They were found to be superior in . . . developing ethnically relevant curricula, using community resources in teaching and initiating contact with parents, [and] bringing about [positive] changes in a child's self-concept. (National Advisory Council 1975, p. 15)

4. Comprehensive Elementary Teacher Education Model (CETEM)

In 1968 the U.S. Office of Education embarked on a major project with several universities and regional education laboratories to improve preservice elementary education. This project was known as the Comprehensive Elementary Teacher Education Model (CETEM) program.

As a result of a national competition, federal monies for Phase 1 were awarded to nine universities, research institutes, and consortia. To be a bidder in the competition, applicants had to indicate that their plan for preservice elementary teacher education would meet the following requirements, among others:

1. The goals or outcomes must be stated in terms of teacher competencies (a portent of competency-based teacher education);

2. The professional education curriculum must be stated explicitly in terms of the teacher competencies;
3. The relationship between the professional education curriculum and the rest of the undergraduate program and the graduates' inservice program must be described;
4. Selection criteria for entry into the preservice program must be explicit;
5. Provisions must be made for follow-up studies of graduates.

An analysis of the professional education curricula in the nine CETEM programs that were undertaken (Cruickshank 1970) found them to contain the following components:

1. Early awareness and engagement, intended to help prospective teachers decide whether a career in teaching was for them;
2. Study of classroom communication using then popular classroom observational systems;
3. Study of and practice in the technical skills of teaching using microteaching;
4. Study of teaching problems and decision making using simulation;
5. Study of self and interpersonal relations using sensitivity training;
6. Child development;
7. Human learning;
8. Study of how knowledge is produced;
9. Study of how to build a curriculum;
10. Diagnosis of learning difficulties;
11. School social and cultural dynamics;
12. Evaluation;
13. Education technology;
14. Role theory;
15. Methods of teaching.

The second phase of CETEM competition resulted in 34 bidders submitting proposals to the federal government. Bidders were required to describe:

a model teacher training program based upon the specifications designed by one or more of the groups engaged in Phase 1. The remainder of the design becomes the design for a feasibility study of developing, implementing and operation. (from the Request for Proposals)

Because of an oversupply of elementary teachers in the 1970s, the federal government did not provide funds to implement any of the CETEM programs. Still, the activities of the first two phases of CETEM generated some new perspectives for the preservice curriculum.

5. *Teachers for the Real World*

In 1966 the U.S. Office of Education, under the National Defense Education Act, Title XI, created the National Institute for Advanced Study in Teaching Disadvantaged Youth. The institute's steering committee soon turned its attention from its stated purpose of preparing teachers to serve disadvantaged youth to one of preparing teachers in general. In *Teachers for the Real World* (Smith, Cohen, and Pearl 1969), the committee stressed the need to prepare teachers with a multicultural point of view.

The committee's proposed program for preservice teacher education has three major components: *theoretical, training, and teaching field.* The *theoretical* component occurs on campus and would help preservice teachers understand *educationally significant events* likely to happen in their K-12 classrooms. Thus if conflict is an expected significant occurrence, then teachers would learn to recognize it, understand its origin and nature, and be in a better position to resolve it.

To provide such a theoretical component requires a series of curriculum development activities. First, significant classroom events must be identified. These might include classroom transitions, alienated children, cheating, off-task behavior, or conflict. Second, original records, or *protocols*, of the events must be prepared. Protocols can be written, videotaped, or audiotaped. Third, the theoretical knowledge that preservice teachers need to know in order to analyze and understand the events depicted in each protocol must be accumulated. Finally, preservice teachers are presented with the protocol and the theoretical knowledge that will illuminate it.

Of course, not all theoretical knowledge can be learned by analyzing protocols of classroom and school life. Thus there also would be courses to teach key concepts from the social and behavioral sciences.

The second curriculum component, *training*, would occur in a public school. Preservice teachers would learn and practice technical skills in real classrooms. Skills might include diagnosing pupil needs, working with learning groups of different sizes, using audiovisual equipment and other technology, and evaluating pupil learning. In addition, preservice teachers would be helped with personal professional problems and sensitized to their own feelings, attitudes, and prejudices. Novice teachers would begin by working with small groups but gradually would take over the entire class.

The *teaching field,* or subject matter preparation, is the third component. Included in this component are the teachers' subject matter content courses, general education, and "knowledge about knowledge." Suggestions are made for improving both content and instruction in this component.

Additional elements of the committee's proposed program include recognition that preservice teachers be allowed to develop a personally comfortable teaching style and to use that style to its best advantage, and that preservice teachers develop an understanding of the principles, policies, and procedures of their organized profession. A paid internship completes the curriculum.

6. *Crisis in the Classroom*

Journalist Charles Silberman was commissioned by the Carnegie Corporation Commission on the Education of Educators to undertake a three-year study of the role of the university in educating educators. His report, *Crisis in the Classroom* (1970), actually concentrates on problems that beset American education generally; but three of his chapters specifically deal with teacher preparation.

Crisis in the Classroom, like Conant's *The Education of American Teachers,* was a best seller that brought the issues and problems of the teacher education curriculum to the direct attention of the general public. Silberman argues that:

> The central task of teacher education . . . is to provide teachers with a sense of purpose . . . with a philosophy of education. This means developing teachers' ability and desire to think seriously, deeply and continuously about the purposes and consequences of what they do. (p. 472)

Silberman argues that teachers must become *students of teaching* more than they must be merely skillful at teaching a discipline. Unless a teacher is also a student of teaching, "he cannot grow as a teacher" (p. 472). Teachers need insights into their purposes as teachers and how these purposes relate to the school as a social setting, to the values of the local community, and to society in general. Teachers must understand human growth and development and the nature of mind and thought. Teachers must gain mastery of subject matter in order to provide "a solid foundation and the knowledge of how to learn whatever else he needs to know as he goes along" (p. 491).

Silberman devotes a full chapter of his book to the liberal education of teachers — one that equips teachers to ask why and to think seriously and deeply about what they are doing. He also makes a case for the foundation areas in professional education. For example, he argues that teachers need to study the history and philosophy of education and that "the study of psychology, sociology and anthropology also deserve a central place in teacher education" (p. 493).

With regard to helping teachers understand themselves, Silberman notes:

> a growing number of educationists . . . are turning to "sensitivity training" as a means of giving . . . teachers a greater awareness of themselves and of others. (p. 499)

7. Teacher Effectiveness Research

During the 1970s there was a renewed interest among researchers in studying classrooms in order to understand what constitutes teacher effectiveness. It was believed that such knowledge could be used to develop a curriculum for a performance-based education of teachers. The movement gained momentum following the release of a study by Rosenshine (1971) and a related piece by Rosenshine and Furst (1971). These two sources contain reviews of 50 studies of teaching that attempt to identify relationships between "process variables," or teacher behaviors, and "product variables," or student achievement. The factors most often associated with student learning were teacher "clarity, variability, enthusiasm, task-oriented or business-like behavior and student opportunity to learn the criterion material."

Dunkin and Biddle, in their milestone book, *A Study of Teaching* (1974), review many clusters of studies that each focus on a common dimension of teacher behavior, such as "teacher talk," or on some classroom phenomenon, such as "classroom management and control." Their review reveals several promising classroom practices, but they caution that many need to be validated experimentally.

In a review of federally funded research on teacher effectiveness, Cruickshank (1976) reports that while some teacher behaviors are effective regardless of the subject or grade level being taught, other teacher behaviors are effective for only a particular grade or subject. Cruickshank argues that part of the teacher education curricula must be specialized in order to prepare teachers to be effective at a particular grade level and with the particular subject matter. Thus special methods classes are necessary.

Subsequently, a large number of researchers examined a wide variety of teacher behaviors. Some of the teacher effectiveness literature that has implications for the teacher preparation curriculum includes: Borich (1979), Brophy (1979), Cruickshank (1990), Doyle (1979, 1983), Gage (1978), Good (1983), Good and McCaslin (1992), Griffin (1983), Medley (1977), Porter and

Brophy (1988), Powell (1978), Soar and Soar (1976), Stallings (1983), and Walberg (1986).

8. School-Based Teacher Education

The Study Commission on Undergraduate Education and the Education of Teachers was established by the U.S. Office of Education in 1972 as a voice for the poor, powerless, and oppressed. The Study Commission, which functioned from 1972 to 1976, was made up of more than 50 persons representing stakeholders in undergraduate teacher education. Its major publications were *Teacher Education in the United States: The Responsibility Gap* (1976), *The University Can't Train Teachers* (Olson, Freeman, Bowman, and Pieper 1972), and *Education for 1984 and After* (Olson, Freeman, and Bowman 1972).

Among the major premises guiding the work of the Study Commission were that: 1) local control of education and teacher education is highly desirable, even necessary; 2) most teacher training should take place in community-controlled schools; 3) education and teacher education must recognize and support cultural pluralism; and 4) teacher training should use a variety of curricula and methods.

Among the suggestions and recommendations related to the preservice curriculum in the final report, *The Responsibility Gap,* are that: 1) preservice teachers should have experiences in local communities; 2) the teacher education curriculum should concentrate more on skills and competencies, sympathy for and understanding of children, and ability to work successfully with others; 3) programs should produce teachers who can work effectively in both classroom and community; 4) the curriculum must prepare teachers for community helping and community building; and 5) the curriculum should offer the preservice teachers "a perspective which might encourage them to change something," and insights "needed to make education serve the interests and survival needs of a child's class, culture and person."

The Study Commission's strong commitment to the concept of school-based teacher education is epitomized in the following statement from *The University Can't Train Teachers:*

> The professional aspect of the training of teachers needs to be centered in the schools and controlled by them as a "technical training" comparable in some ways to industrial training. The role of higher education in the education of teachers may be to provide a good general or liberal education in the first three years of college. School-based professional training should be offered in the fourth and possibly fifth years. . . . School-based professional training should include a strong component of teaching by the community, and control by parents and students. It should respect the life-style, value system, language and expressive system of the culture in which the school which provides training is located: both teacher trainees and the IHE training faculty should respond to these cultur[al] aspects. (p. vi)

The work of the Study Commission reflects the social unrest in America in the 1960s and 1970s. Such concerns were recognized by persons in teacher education, but whether this recognition was sufficient is another matter. With the shortfall in federal and state funds to support teacher education, the concept of "teacher as community builder," which was central to this reform effort, seemed to be displaced by other urgent economic and political challenges.

9. Promoting Cultural Pluralism

The 1960s and 1970s in America was a period of social and political ferment. It was the time of "movements" to elevate the status of African Americans, Mexican Americans, Native Americans, women, homosexuals, and the handicapped. The mood of the times was that everyone matters, everyone counts! Among these various movements one was aimed primarily at the education establishment; this was multicultural education, which was intended to enhance the self-concepts of all minority children in America's classrooms by establishing that their cultures are worthy and, in fact, exemplary. It also intended to inform majority children that minorities had made significant contributions to American life.

> Multicultural education recognizes cultural diversity as a fact of life in American Society, and it affirms that this cultural diversity is a valuable resource that should be preserved and extended. (Hidalgo 1973, p. 264)

The long-range outcome was to be the positive transformation of attitudes of members of the dominant culture toward minorities. The immediate task for teachers was to teach all children to know and respect all Americans. The impact of the multicultural movement on public school education was broad. Among other things, schools were urged to:

1. Examine texts for evidence of racism, classism, and sexism;
2. Develop new curricula providing opportunities to learn about and interact with a variety of cultural groups;
3. Organize the curriculum around universal human concerns that bring cultural perspectives to bear on issues;
4. Create school environments that radiate cultural diversity; and
5. Recognize, accept, and use bilingualism as a positive contribution.

The multicultural movement has had a considerable impact on teacher education. For example, the 1982 National Council for Accreditation of Teacher Education (NCATE) *Standards* required that:

> The institution provides for multicultural education in its teacher education curricula, including both the general and professional studies components. (p. 14)

Further, NCATE suggested that the multicultural education of teachers include experiences for preservice teachers that:

> (1) promote analytical and evaluative abilities to confront issues such as participatory democracy, racism and sexism, and parity of power; (2) develop skills for values clarification

including the study of the manifest and latent transmissions of values; (3) examine the dynamics of diverse cultures and the implications for developing teaching strategies; and (4) examine linguistic variations and diverse learning styles as a basis for the development of appropriate teaching strategies. (p. 14)

The Philosophy of Education Society also supported "selected and appropriate elements related to multicultural education . . . in teacher education programs" (Philosophy of Education Society 1980).

Other support for the multicultural teacher education movement includes: the publication by the AACTE Commission on Multicultural Education and the Committee on Performance-Based Teacher Education of the book, *Multicultural Education Through Competency-Based Education* (Hunter 1974); establishment of the AACTE Ethnic Heritage Center for Teacher Education with support from Title IX of the Elementary and Secondary Education Act; and related revisions of various state teacher education standards. The Teacher Corps and the Higher Education Act of 1965 also promoted acceptance of cultural diversity.

Arciniega (1977) offers teacher educators a profile of an ideal teacher of multicultural education. Among other things, he calls for preparing teachers who believe cultural diversity is worthy, who have a commitment to enhancing the minority child's self-image, who have confidence in culturally different children's ability to learn, who possess knowledge of culturally and linguistically different children, who have literacy in a minority language or dialect, who have skill in successful approaches to teaching culturally different students, and who are willing to participate in minority community activities.

By 1978, many colleges and universities reported that they included multicultural education in the preservice curriculum (Commission on Multicultural Education 1978). On the other hand, Banks (1977) has noted:

There has been little calm and serious public debate concerning multiethnic education among educators. Why?

There is certainly no lack of divergent beliefs. . . . The answer lies . . . in the explosiveness of the topic. The ethnic studies movement was born in the midst of a highly politicized and radically tense period. Scholars and educators have allowed strong emotions to overwhelm them in discussions of ethnicity and schooling. (p. 695)

By the 1980s, the social consciousness of American education caused multicultural education to be more inclusive of all types of diversity, including exceptionality. The 1990 NCATE *Standards* noted:

The professional studies component(s) for the preparation of teachers provides knowledge about and appropriate skills in . . . cultural influences on learning [and] instructional strategies for exceptionalities. . . . The unit provides for study and experiences that help education students understand and apply appropriate strategies for individual learning needs, especially culturally diverse and exceptional populations. . . . The curriculum for professional studies component(s) incorporates multicultural and global perspectives; and that Education students participate in field-based and/or clinical experiences with culturally diverse and exceptional populations. (pp. 40-41)

The 1995 version of the NCATE *Standards* requires teacher preparation to attend to issues and aspects of cultural diversity and exceptionality throughout professional studies. Whereas universities merely instituted a single course or unit in order to comply with the 1990 standards, now multiculturalism-diversity must be addressed throughout the program.

10. Teaching as Artistry

In the 1960s and 1970s, Arthur Combs and others advocated a highly personal, idiosyncratic view of teaching. They shunned the view that good teachers are generally alike, contrary to the research on teacher effectiveness.

The good teacher is *not* one who behaves in a given way. He is an artist, skillful in facilitating effective growth in students. To accomplish this he must use methods appropriate to the complex circumstances he is involved in. His methods must fit the goals he seeks, the children he is working with, the philosophy he is guided by. . . . The good teacher is no carbon copy but possesses something intensely and personally his own. (Combs et al. 1974, pp. 7, 8)

For Combs and his associates the task of the teacher education curriculum is to assist the preservice teacher in "becoming," that is, learning how to use "self-as-instrument."

Advocates of the self-as-instrument concept eschew stimulus-response psychology and psychoanalytic theories because they lead to mechanistic and atomistic ways of working with persons. Rather, they embrace what is called "Third Force" psychology, which regards humans not as things to be manipulated and molded, but as organisms in the process of self-development and becoming. Third Force psychologists believe that teacher preparation should be concerned primarily with helping preservice teachers to be in touch with themselves — their feelings, attitudes, and beliefs about subject matter, people, and purposes of learning. This preservice teacher preparation curriculum would involve students in continuous exploration of self and others, ideas and purposes, as they relate to problems of the classroom. This ongoing exploration would include learning experiences that confront preservice teachers with professional problems and engage them in personal decision making to find solutions (Combs 1978, p. 560). Personal discovery would be enhanced through counseling, group experiences, sensitivity training, and other awareness techniques.

In the 1970s the University of Florida initiated such a preservice program with Combs as its architect. The program centered on three kinds of experiences: 1) field experiences that provided early and continuous exposure to children and youth in natural classrooms and in the community, 2) "substantive panels" that offered broad exposure to ideas through individual and group study and interaction with faculty specialists, and 3) the seminar, in which a stable, base group explored the personal meaning of

59

experiences encountered during the process of becoming a teacher.

The university's field experience program began with the pre-service teacher working with one or a few children for four hours a week and continued for at least four quarters, with increasing responsibility until the novice finally assumed the role of a full-time teacher. Throughout their varied field experiences, preservice teachers were exposed to different types of teaching and class-room organization, interacted with diverse students of different ages, and experienced life in the community.

Substantive panels were intended to expose preservice teachers to professional ideas. A panel, staffed by regular faculty, pro-vided sessions that stimulated preservice students to think about professional information and techniques in their special areas of interest. The panels began with orientation sessions that explained how students could proceed to study in their area and were fol-lowed with optional small-group meetings and individual confer-ences. Then students, either independently or in small groups, developed work contracts that were negotiated with the faculty.

Each seminar served as the home base for 30 preservice teach-ers and one faculty member. The primary purpose of the seminars was to create a setting in which students could discover personal meaning for the ideas and experiences to which they recently had been exposed.

Experiential learning was emphasized throughout the Florida program. Teacher education faculty were not so much teachers as counselors, skilled in helping each student find out how best to become a unique helper of children and a classroom artist.

What distinguished the preservice teacher education formulated by Combs and his associates is its greater attention to *how* the professional curriculum should be presented.

11. Performance/Competency-Based Teacher Education

Performance- or competency-based teacher education (CBTE) was a major national effort at curriculum reform. It had its origins in the Comprehensive Elementary Teacher Education Model (CETEM) and was supported by the Educational Testing Service National Commission on Performance-Based Education (McDonald 1974) and the AACTE Committee on Performance-Based Teacher Education (1974). Among other things, CBTE was an effort to identify the critical abilities and skills, or competencies, of teaching and to direct the teacher preparation curriculum toward the attainment of those competencies.

Several ways of identifying these competencies were proposed: l) they could be gleaned from research on teaching effectiveness; 2) they could be provided by experienced, expert educators; 3) they could be derived from polls of various stakeholders in education; 4) they could be culled from the literature; 5) they could be extracted from different teacher roles; and 6) they could result from task analyses of teaching at different grade levels and in different curriculum areas. All of these approaches were used, resulting in numerous competency lists, for example, *Florida Catalog of Teacher Competencies* (Dodl et al. 1972) and *Generic Teaching Competencies* (Pennsylvania Department of Education 1973).

Once identified and agreed on, the competencies are stated in terms of observable teacher behaviors. Next, curriculum materials, or *learning modules*, are developed. Modules normally include performance objectives, references, equipment, materials needed, alternate learning experiences, and supplements. Through the use of such modules, the preservice teacher is expected to be able to perform one or more competencies.

The broad categories of competencies included in the modules cover such areas as planning instruction, implementing instruction, assessing and evaluating student behavior, performing administrative duties, communicating verbally and nonverbally, and developing personal skills (Dodl et al. 1972, p. 6).

With its emphasis on identifying and gaining consensus on requisite teacher abilities, the CBTE movement was a major influence on preservice curriculum development and later provided the impetus for the teacher competency testing movement.

12. Personalized Teacher Education (PTE)

Frances Fuller and others at the Research and Development Center for Teacher Education at the University of Texas believed that some of the traditional preservice curriculum does not match the psychological needs of preservice students (Fuller and Bown 1975). She argued that preservice students sometimes complain that certain education courses are not relevant because these students are not ready to benefit from some of them.

From her research, Fuller concluded that "beginning teachers are concerned about class control, about their own content adequacy, about the situations in which they teach and about evaluations by their supervisors, by their pupils" (1969, p. 216). Unfortunately, preservice students' concerns are not commonly addressed in education courses.

Beginning student teachers are specifically "concerned with the parameters of the new school situation and with discipline." As student teaching progresses, their concerns shift to their students and how well they are learning (1969, p. 211).

Consequently, Fuller and her associates advocated a Personalized Teacher Education (PTE) program (Fuller 1974). That program would use a sequential curriculum to match the student's personal and professional development. The curriculum first focuses on concerns about self, then moves to concerns about the teaching task, and finally focuses on concerns for pupils.

In order to implement PTE, a considerable amount of personal information about preservice students must be collected. This information can be collected through self-reports, psychological instruments, and self-observations involving videotaping. Once the information is collected, it is presented to a student in such a way that the student can observe discrepancies between self-perceptions, observation of actual behavior, and some standard of performance. The intent always is to use the information to move the student toward the higher phase of teaching concerns, that is, toward concern for students. Thus the goal of PTE is to give each prospective teacher a personalized education, so the teacher in turn can provide one for learners.

13. The Teacher as Actor

Robert Travers suggests that it is not enough for preservice students merely to know *what* roles and abilities they must acquire in order to become effective classroom performers (Travers 1975; Travers and Dillon 1975). They also must learn *how* to acquire them. Travers turned to the work of the famous Russian director Stanislavski, the founder of method acting. Stanislavski's work appealed to Travers because it called for the actor to become totally immersed in a role, rather than merely saying the correct words and performing required actions. Similarly, to be an effective teacher, the preservice student has to become completely immersed in that role.

To immerse preservice students in the role of effective teacher, Travers borrows a five-step procedure from Stanislavski:

1. Study the role.
2. Search for material through which the role can be achieved.
3. Search for role sources within the individual.
4. Prepare to enter the classroom.
5. Search for creative ways to keep the role alive.

Study the Role. Preservice students first have to understand what roles and abilities they must acquire in order to become effective teachers. Travers is critical of the customary practice of sending students into natural classrooms to observe teachers, because the role model they observe may be a negative one. Instead, he proposes using carefully selected film clips of effective teachers who demonstrate the roles and abilities that contribute to their success. By viewing and then analyzing such films, the preservice teacher can then speculate about how the effective teacher might feel and behave under numerous other circumstances.

Search for Material. Preservice teachers must be exposed to exemplars of teaching both as role models and as a source of ideas. However, they must be warned against merely attempting to copy the role modeled by a particular teacher. Instead, they must understand the nature and the problems of teaching and discover some of the techniques and resources that they can adapt for themselves.

Search for Role Sources. An attribute of effective teachers is clarity. Teachers cannot pretend to be clear. If they are not clear, they must learn how to become so, or else choose a profession other than teaching. Once a personal, authentic role of teaching has been identified, then preservice students must find within themselves the aptitudes needed for assuming the role.

Prepare to Enter the Classroom. Travers suggests that the first thing novice teachers must learn to do on entering a classroom is to become comfortable. When that is achieved, they should have opportunities for nonstressful interactions with the entire class. This gradual induction into the dynamics of a classroom provides time during which novices can practice their roles with increasingly larger numbers of pupils. Travers calls for a mentor, or "role trainer," to help the novice gain insight into role development and performance. The trainer would be akin to an acting coach.

Search for Creative Ways to Keep the Role Alive. Travers sees teaching as a developmental process that needs continuing nurturance. Teachers must be ever-ready to modify their role and to search for material and for sources within themselves through which the modified role can be achieved.

14. *Educating a Profession*

Educating a Profession (Howsam et al. 1976), the report by AACTE's Bicentennial Commission on Education for the Profession of Teaching, was an effort to stimulate discussion on several aspects of teacher preparation, including the curriculum. Urging that "the profession must establish consensus on the professional culture required to *begin* the practice of teaching," the report suggests 11 major curriculum components:

1. General or liberal studies.
2. Education in the disciplines that provide much of the theoretical base for educational practice, for example, psychology, sociology, anthropology, and philosophy.

64

3. Preparation in an academic specialization (content specialty).
4. Foundations of education that illuminate education issues and problems and that develop a sense of social purpose.
5. The professional knowledge base needed to understand and analyze life in classrooms.
6. Generic teaching behaviors and skills.
7. Teacher values and attitudes "to provide preservice teachers with a philosophy of education that will help them to think seriously . . . about the purposes and consequences of what they do" (p. 89).
8. Professional literacy or knowledge about educational and sociopolitical issues.
9. Field experiences that relate theory and practice.
10. Preparation to work with disabled children.
11. Study of a significant subculture.

The Howsam report did stimulate discussion and debate and has since been followed by numerous reform proposals with similar themes.

15. Reflective Teaching and Simulation

Reflective Teaching (Cruickshank et al. 1980, 1991) is designed to make preservice students more thoughtful and wise about their teaching. It is intended to help preservice teachers develop higher level professional cognitive skills, namely, analysis, synthesis, evaluation, and problem solving.

The intention is to make preservice students more thoughtful and perceptive practitioners as a consequence of contemplating their teaching. The program includes a number of specially developed, brief lessons that preservice teachers teach to peers. After several preservice students teach one of the lessons to a small group of their peers, each teacher and the group of peer learners use guided discussion to reflect on the teaching process and its results. The college instructor continues the discussion by focusing on the question: What have we learned about teaching and learning?

Cruickshank and his colleagues also developed two simulations based on information gathered from practicing K-12 teachers. These simulations present the most frequent and most bothersome problems teachers face in the classroom (Cruickshank, Broadbent, and Bubb 1967; Cruickshank and Leonard 1967; Cruickshank and Broadbent 1968; Cruickshank, Kennedy, Leonard, and Thurman 1968; Cruickshank 1969; Cruickshank, Kennedy, and Myers 1974; Bainer 1986). In each simulation, participants assume the role of a new teacher. Following an orientation to the school and school district where they would work, they are given pupil cumulative record folders and other job-related information. After assimilating such information, participants are exposed to a number of the classroom problems, which may be portrayed on film, in role plays, or in written incidents. The participants' task is to try to resolve each problem in order to reach the desired goal with the fewest negative effects for others (pupils, parents, administrator, or other teachers).

Relatedly, Cruickshank, Applegate, Holton, Mager, Myers, Novak, and Tracey (1980) identified and organized the education theory associated with five prevalent areas of teacher concern: affiliation, control, parent relationships and home conditions, student success, and time management. Direct engagement with these concerns and exposure to the knowledge related to them is intended to help preservice students become aware of the more difficult and challenging aspects of classroom life and, more important, to help them approach such situations with a problem-solving attitude.

16. Schools of Pedagogy

Eleven years after publication of *Teachers for the Real World* (Smith, Cohen, and Pearl 1969), B.O. Smith and his colleagues at the University of South Florida presented a second plan for teacher preparation, *A Design for a School of Pedagogy* (Smith, Silverman, Borg, and Fry 1980). As the title implies, *A Design for a School of Pedagogy* suggests the creation of new schools of pedagogy to correct the inadequacies of current university-based teacher education.

Among its many proposals, the authors recommend that prospective teachers follow the four-year bachelor's degree program with two years in a school of pedagogy leading to a master of pedagogy degree. In the bachelor's degree program, the major focus would be on preparing teachers in the subjects they will teach and "complementary subjects" for both prospective secondary and elementary teachers. In addition, the students would receive a solid background in the social and behavioral sciences underlying pedagogy.

In the school of pedagogy, the entire graduate curriculum focus would be on the science and art of teaching. Areas covered during the fifth and sixth years include: clinical observation, exceptionality, pedagogical psychology, measurement and evaluation, school and community, curriculum and instruction, content selection and organization, selection of curriculum materials, specialized courses in specific curriculum areas, clinical field experiences, clinical seminars using protocols, and student evaluation and remediation.

According to the authors, if such six-year preservice programs were established, much could be done to right the conditions that have deprofessionalized teacher preparation. Specifically, these new programs would be able to draw on the research on school and teacher effectiveness.

A Design for a School of Pedagogy seems to be the basis for statewide renewal of teacher education in Florida. Indeed, many of its ideas are mimicked in the Holmes Group proposal described later.

17. The NEA Plan

The organized teaching profession itself became involved in the preservice curriculum with the publication of the National Education Association's *Excellence in Our Schools: Teacher Education, An Action Plan* (1982). NEA argued that "Teacher education programs must be designed and developed based on what the practitioner says needs to be known and done for beginning effective practice" (p. 7). Regarding the teacher education curriculum, the report notes:

> All teacher education programs should have three integrated components: liberal arts, at least one subject or teaching specialty, and a professional curriculum. . . . The professional component should focus on classroom practice. Field-based experiences related to all components should be provided throughout the preservice program. (p. 10)

Excellence goes on to describe three critical functions of teaching that must be the basis for the design, development, and implementation of college programs preparing teachers; it presents illustrations of what teachers must know or be able to do in order to perform the above three functions; and it provides lists of learnings, skills, and field-based experiences related to the three major functions.

According to the NEA, the three major functions of teaching are facilitating learning, managing the classroom, and making professional decisions. These three teaching functions are translated into learnings and skills and suggest that the curriculum focus on the following:

1. Human growth and development
2. Content studies
3. Human behavior
4. Learning
5. Exceptionality
6. Assessment
7. Social, cultural, and environmental effects on learning
8. Communication
9. Instructional design
10. Professional resources and materials
11. Design and evaluation of learning activities
12. Legal responsibilities of teachers
13. Foundations of public schooling

14. Group dynamics
15. The politics of education
16. Creating and using student records
17. Education research and its interpretation

In addition, the NEA report recommends a variety of field-based or campus-based laboratory and clinical experiences, including:

1. Observing students, classrooms, teacher conferences, school board meetings, state education department activities, state legislature, professional and learned organizations, and the organized teaching profession;
2. Microteaching and mirror teaching;
3. Developing case studies of individual students;
4. Translating education theory into classroom practice;
5. Participating in curriculum design and development;
6. Using instructional technology; and
7. Classroom teaching.

18. The Paideia Proposal

The Paideia Proposal: An Educational Manifesto (1982) by philosopher Mortimer Adler is a plan to reform the K-12 curriculum. However, it has clear implications for the preparation of teachers. The Adler plan calls for a single-track, K-12 academic program with virtually no electives nor vocational preparation. The proposed curriculum is based on three types of learning that would occur simultaneously in all grades: acquisition of organized knowledge, development of intellectual skills, and enlarged understanding of ideas and values.

A central premise of Adler's *Paideia Proposal* is that American education is failing, but it can be restored by getting back to the basics. A. Graham Down, executive director of the Council for Basic Education, notes:

> The Paideia Proposal embodies accurately the conception of education the Council for Basic Education has promoted. . . . There are three premises: the principal purpose

of schooling is academic, not social; some subjects are more important than others; and all can learn regardless of social or economic background. (*ASCD Update*, March 1983, p. 4)

Adler feels strongly that current teacher candidates are unsuited to learn the new curriculum and that current programs in schools of education are unsuited to prepare persons to teach it. Says Adler, "I would abolish all schools of education" (Buckley 1982, p. 30). Adler argues that while we are educating a new generation of teachers in the three primary elements of learning, we must select teachers who are "on the way" to becoming educated persons. According to Adler, these people can be identified because they manifest competence as learners, show strong interest in their personal education, and are motivated to continue learning while teaching.

Adler would require all prospective teachers to take four years of college, in which the courses "would be mainly liberal, humanistic in general." He also "would require of every future teacher that he have three years of clinical practice . . . teaching under supervision — because teaching is an art that requires coaching" (Buckley 1982, p. 30). Adler claims:

All skills of teaching are intellectual skills that can be developed only by coaching, not by lecture courses in pedagogy and teaching methods such as are now taught in most schools or departments of education and are now required for certification. (Buckley 1982, p. 61)

In November 1994, *Education Week* listed two national organizations that continue to disseminate information and prepare educators in the Paideia principles: the National Paideia Center at the University of North Carolina at Chapel Hill and the Paideia Group, also in Chapel Hill.

19. Readying the Beginning Teacher

Scannell and his colleagues, two of whom had worked on the AACTE bicentennial publication, *Educating a Profession* (Howsam et al. 1976), prepared a follow-up publication, the purpose of

70

which was to define "what teacher characteristics should be guaranteed upon graduation from a teacher education program" and what curriculum would promote development of such characteristics. The publication, *Educating a Profession. Profile of a Beginning Teacher* (Scannell et al. 1983), calls for the preservice curriculum to be organized into four components: general education, preprofessional study in the disciplines undergirding pedagogy, academic specialization, and professional study.

Under *general education,* the proposed curriculum would result in proficiency in the art of communication. Specifically, preservice students would be: 1) expert in the communication arts (reading, writing, speaking, listening, creative expression, and forms of nonverbal communication); 2) top flight in mathematical skills; 3) masterful in understanding the nature, evolution, and uses of language and how language reflects culture; and 4) adept in understanding the function, use, and effects of mass communications, the computer, and other technology. In addition, preservice teachers would understand groups and institutions, principles of physical and mental health, the relationship between society and work, the relationship of nature and the universe, the relationship of new technologies to human nature, the relationship of time and civilization to values and beliefs, and the fine arts.

Under *preprofessional study* in the disciplines undergirding pedagogy, preservice teachers would "acquire an adequate theoretical foundation in the undergirding disciplines, primarily the social and behavioral sciences such as anthropology, philosophy and sociology." Such study would permit prospective teachers to understand principles and methods of inquiry related to education and teaching, to understand factors fostering or inhibiting communication, and to know something of the basic disciplines from which teachers draw experience and knowledge.

Under *academic specialization*, preservice teachers would study the subjects they eventually would teach. The focus of these content studies would be on "the nature of knowledge, the structure of the discipline and the relationship between them, and the processes of inquiry and research."

Under *professional studies or pedagogy,* the curriculum would consist of four subparts: foundational studies in education, generic teaching knowledge and skills, specialized pedagogical knowledge and skills, and field and clinical laboratory experience.

Many of the recommendations in *Profile of a Beginning Teacher* reflected the current thinking on the teacher education curriculum, were similar to those contained in the 1982 NCATE *Standards,* and were very similar, as would be expected, to Howsam et al. (1976). However, focus in the Scannell report was on the concept of generic teaching behaviors and on sequentially planned campus and field-based laboratory experiences.

20. A Dean's Proposal

Hendrik Gideonse, former dean of the College of Education at the University of Cincinnati, suggests that there are three essential components to the professional education of teachers:

> The first is a sound liberal education and thorough mastery over the content areas to be taught. The second . . . is a thorough exposure to those domains of knowledge and inquiry . . . that inform about the nature of humanity, society and culture. Third, the growing body of professional knowledge . . . must also be mastered. (Gideonse 1982, p. 15)

Gideonse includes literacy, communication and cognitive skills, aesthetics, and values in the liberal education component. The domains of knowledge and inquiry include study in the humanities and the behavioral and social sciences, because they "define the nature of human development and learning . . . help establish the cultural contexts within which educational goals are defined and served" (pp. 15-16).

Gideonse suggests the following curriculum to meet the need for professional knowledge:

1. Instructional alternatives, including use of media;
2. Learner and learning differences;
3. Instruction for specific needs of individual learners;
4. Curriculum theory;

5. Small-group process;
6. Professional responsibilities;
7. School faculty and staff roles and their interrelationships;
8. Parent relationships;
9. Classroom management; and
10. Self-awareness.

21. *A Call for Change*

A Call for Change in Teacher Education (National Commission for Excellence in Teacher Education 1985) was developed as a reply to the highly censorious report on public school education, *A Nation at Risk* (National Commission on Excellence in Education 1983). *A Call for Change* addresses many issues in teacher preparation, including "teacher supply and demand, accountability, resources, and necessary conditions."

The authors assume that teacher education will continue to be centered in colleges and universities. Thus they argue that "it is essential that higher education institutions strengthen their commitments to the preparation of excellent teachers. We also believe that the connections between colleges and schools should be significantly improved" (p. 2).

The authors propose teacher education programs that include liberal education, concentrated subject specialization, and systematic study and application of pedagogy (p. 11). They argue that the liberal education of preservice teachers should be at least as extensive as that received by students in general and that such courses should include sociology, anthropology, and psychology. In addition, they recommend that prospective secondary teachers major in two subject specializations, while elementary candidates should have an extended general education program and courses in child development.

With regard to professional education, *A Call for Change* cites the need for prospective teachers to:

• Understand how to select and present appropriate content.
• Recognize errors and difficulties students experience.

- Know how to reteach.
- Understand how individuals think and learn at different ages and stages.
- Select, develop, and use appropriate teaching strategies and materials.
- Observe and analyze student performance.
- Conduct discussions and seminars.
- Know and utilize what is known about effective teaching and schooling.
- Be able to integrate technology.
- Apply appropriate ideas and facts learned in advanced academic courses (pp. 11-12).

All of this coursework should be accompanied by on-campus laboratory experiences and work in the field. And, conversely, all work in the field should be the focus of seminars. The report states that prospective teachers must have teaching experiences "in real and simulated circumstances." Some of that teaching should be videotaped; and all teaching practice should be subjected to detailed, repeated analysis and criticism by the preservice teacher and mentors.

One conclusion reached in the report is that in order to prepare teachers as well as we know how, preparation programs may have to be extended and new teachers required to complete a paid, on-the-job internship.

22. The Carnegie Foundation's Proposals

The Carnegie Foundation issued several reports during the 1980s that have ramifications for teacher preparation, including *High School: A Report on Secondary Education in America* (1983); *A Nation Prepared: Teachers for the 21st Century* (1986); and *Turning Points: Preparing American Youth for the 21st Century* (1989).

The final report of a three-year study of 16,000 public high schools, *High School: A Report on Secondary Education in America* (Boyer 1983) dealt with the high school curriculum.

74

However, it also called for sweeping reform in teacher preparation programs. Boyer recommends the following:

1. Preservice secondary school teachers should study a common core of subjects paralleling the high school curriculum proposed in the report.
2. Preservice teachers should complete a major in an academic discipline, and significant opportunity for classroom observation should be provided. Prospective teachers should major in an academic subject, not in education.
3. Preservice teachers should have a fifth year of combined instructional and apprenticeship experiences that includes a core of four courses designed to meet the special needs of educators. The proposed courses are Schooling in America, Learning Theory and Research, Teaching of Writing, and Use of Technology. The crucial apprenticeship experience would be with a team of master teachers.

Finally, the *High School* report called for a series of one-day Common Learning Seminars to be held during the fifth year, in which preservice teachers would meet outstanding scholar-teachers in the arts and sciences who would relate the knowledge of their fields to contemporary political and social events.

In *A Nation Prepared: Teachers for the 21st Century* (1986), the Carnegie Task Force on Teaching as a Profession examined teaching as a profession. This proposal calls for:

1. Development of new framework for teaching;
2. Higher professional standards;
3. Restructuring the teaching force by such means as differential staffing; and
4. Increasing subject matter preparation of prospective teachers.

A Nation Prepared recommends that a bachelor's degree in the arts and sciences be a prerequisite for professional study in teaching. In addition, it promotes a new professional curriculum in graduate schools of education leading to a Master of Teaching degree. The proposed curriculum would be based on systematic study of knowledge about teaching and include an internship and residency in schools.

The Carnegie Task Force on Teaching as a Profession also recommended the establishment of a national board to certify teachers, a proposal that has resulted in the National Board of Professional Teaching Standards (NBPTS). The primary goal of the board is to restore public confidence in the nation's schools. The explicit purpose of this board is to codify what teachers should know and be able to do and then to "nationally certify" teachers who demonstrate that knowledge and skill.

Finally, the Carnegie Council on Adolescent Development published *Turning Points: Preparing American Youth for the 21st Century* (1989). *Turning Points* is seen as a confirmation of the grassroots movement calling for curricular reform in teacher preparation, particularly as it pertains to preparing middle-level teachers. Describing the issues and problems of adolescence by employing stark and alarming statistics, the document makes eight recommendations for transforming middle schools to meet the developmental needs of the learner. One recommendation is to "staff middle grade schools with teachers who are expert at teaching young adolescents and who have been specially prepared for assignments to the middle grades" (p. 9). The document calls for state licensure and certification or endorsements to address the specialized talents and training of teachers of young adolescents.

23. The Holmes Group

In 1983, then-U.S. Secretary of Education Terrel Bell, several foundations, and the education deans of several "research" universities formed a consortium known as the Holmes Group, which was dedicated to solving problems associated with the perceived low quality of teacher preparation in the United States. In time, more than 100 research institutions were invited to join this group.

In the three years of initial discussions, twin goals were identified by the consortium: the reform of teacher education programs and the reform of the teaching profession generally. The report that emerged after those initial discussions, *Tomorrow's Teachers* (1986), called for extended teacher education programs where, as in Smith et al. (1980) and the Carnegie reports, the professional education of teachers would occur in a postgraduate, master's degree program following a four-year baccalaureate degree. Specifically, the report enumerated six goals related to teacher preparation:

1. Undergraduate prospective teachers cannot major in education. Instead, they pursue more serious general/liberal study and an academic subject normally taught in schools.
2. Prospective career teachers require a master's degree in education and a successful year of well-supervised internship.
3. The curriculum for elementary career teachers would include multiple areas of concentration (each equivalent to a minor) in the subjects for which teachers assume general teaching authority and responsibility.
4. The curriculum for secondary career teachers would include significant graduate study in their major teaching field and areas of concentration in all other subjects they would teach.
5. The curriculum for all prospective career teachers would include substantial knowledge and skill regarding appropriate policy and practice in teaching students with special needs. Advanced graduate study would be required for career professional roles in special education.
6. Teachers who wish to attain career professional status require advanced study appropriate for specialized work in education with other adult professionals (pp. 94-96).

In addition, the Holmes Group called for a change in the "working relationships, roles, and responsibilities within and between schools and universities so that their collaborative endeavors can assure the public of well-educated teachers for America's children" (p. 87). Much of the collaboration was to take place in Professional Development Schools (PDS), which also would be the site for many clinical and laboratory experiences.

The Holmes Group published an additional report focusing on schools of education, *Tomorrow's Schools of Education* (1995). That report includes various goals, including a recommendation that schools of education provide a "common core" of knowledge to both entry-level and advanced students. That core knowledge would include studies of human development and learning; subject matter and pedagogy; instructional management; inquiry, reflection, and research and development; and collaboration in support of young people's learning. This core of knowledge, it is proposed, would increase and deepen as educators continue their professional studies beyond the initial preparation program.

24. The 21st Century Report

The Association of Teacher Educators (ATE) published an agenda of specific recommendations for all primary stakeholders in teacher education: colleges and universities, schools, states and their agencies, and professional organizations. That document, *Restructuring the Education of Teachers: The 21st Century* (1991), listed detailed recommendations under five broad headings:

1. Improving the teacher recruitment and selection processes.
2. Strengthening initial teacher preparation.
3. Facilitating successful entry into the profession.
4. Increasing the capacity for continued professional development.
5. Expanding and employing the research base for teaching and teacher education.

Two of the above areas, strengthening initial teacher preparation and expanding and employing the research base for teaching and teacher education, have a direct impact on the teacher education curriculum.

The report focuses on identifying core pedagogical knowledge in order to strengthen initial teacher preparation. In addition, the report emphasizes collaboration between schools, colleges, state

78

agencies, and professional organizations as a means of strengthening teacher preparation programs. The report supports the Holmes Group recommendation for professional development schools. It also calls for support of and direct involvement in research activities by all primary professional stakeholders.

25. The Renaissance Group

The Renaissance Group, a consortium of 19 universities, was established in 1989 to improve the preparation of teachers on member campuses and to facilitate reform efforts nationally. The contention of this group is that socioeconomic conditions have changed the character of many American classrooms and have impeded effective teaching and learning.

In *Educating the New American Student* (1993), the Renaissance Group focuses on five areas: early childhood education, science and mathematics education, minority and multicultural programs, instructional technology, and interagency collaboration. Within these five areas, the Renaissance Group outlines 12 broad principles that would influence teacher preparation. The principles that would appear to have the most direct influence on the teacher preparation curriculum are:

1. The education of teachers is an all-campus responsibility.
2. Decisions concerning the education of teachers are the shared responsibility of the university faculty, practitioners, and other professionals.
3. The initial preparation of teachers is integrated throughout a student's university experience and is not segmented or reserved to the student's final year.
4. Rigorous learning experiences and exit requirements characterize the program to educate teachers.
5. The academic preparation of teachers includes a rigorous general education program, in-depth subject matter preparation, and both general and content-specific preparation in teaching methodology.

6. Teacher education programs reflect American diversity and prepare graduates to teach in a pluralistic and multicultural society.
7. The education of teachers incorporates extensive and sequenced field and clinical experiences.

26. Project 30

Project 30, sponsored by the Carnegie Foundation of New York, is a collaborative effort involving 30 institutions of higher education across the United States. Its mandate is to redesign the way prospective teachers are educated. The Project 30 reform document calls for joint efforts by the faculties of arts and sciences and the faculties of education to bring about fundamental reform in the preparation of teachers. The report recommends using collaborative curriculum redesign efforts to integrate the liberal arts and education curricula, to strengthen foundations in the arts and sciences, and to improve articulation among those areas and pedagogical study. Doing so, Project 30 contends, will result in better educated, better prepared teachers.

In its report, *The Reform of Teacher Education for the 21st Century: Project 30 Year One Report* (Murray and Fallon 1989), five themes or "conversation topics" for redesigning teacher preparation and its curriculum emerge as foci for action. They are:

1. Subject matter understanding;
2. General and liberal knowledge;
3. Pedagogical content knowledge;
4. Multicultural, international, and other human perspectives; and
5. Recruitment into teaching.

27. Teach for America

The brainchild of Wendy Kopp, "Teach for America" is an alternative route to teaching that has captured the attention of corporations and educators since the early 1990s. Kopp, then a Princeton University student, conceived the idea of a Peace Corps for teachers. With initial support from the Mobil Foundation, she began to recruit outstanding recent college graduates who otherwise might not have considered teaching. These individuals undergo an intensive eight-week summer preparation program and commit to two years of teaching in urban or rural public school districts. To accomplish its goals, Teach for America has taken advantage of state provisions that allow individuals to begin teaching without full certification.

The Teach for America summer training program is located at six school sites. Each school's director and faculty are responsible for designing a curriculum that ensures that 10 broad goals are met. These goals state that Teacher Corps members, on completion of the training, should have developed the ability to:

1. Develop, use, internalize, and understand the rationale behind an ongoing planning and organizational system;
2. Determine the developmental levels — physical, emotional, social, and cognitive — of students, including the ability to recognize exceptionalities and diverse learning styles;
3. Plan a variety of instructional strategies that take into account the learning styles and developmental needs of a diverse student population;
4. Develop and understand the rationale behind behavior management systems and procedures;
5. Develop effective communication strategies and skills;
6. Understand and construct appropriate assessment strategies;
7. Arrange a classroom;
8. Access resources;
9. Refer students to in-school and community support services; and
10. Invest parents or guardians in the education of their children.

Teach for America, as have most alternative routes to teaching, has been criticized by the education community (see Schorr

81

1993). The common thread of criticism is the apparent dearth of professional preparation and training. According to Linda Darling-Hammond (1994), the summer institute offers "no systematic curriculum, no continuous faculty, no guaranteed resources for student learning, and no quality control over school placements, mentoring, or assessment." It appears that until some "official" professional curriculum is made available for scrutiny, Teach for America will be viewed with skepticism.

28. The Network for Educational Renewal

The National Network for Educational Renewal (NNER), founded by John Goodlad, focuses on the simultaneous renewal of schooling and education of educators. Goodlad, in *Teachers for Our Nation's Schools* (1990), reports the conclusions of a five-year study conducted at six representative colleges and universities that prepare teachers. The report draws its conclusions from interviews, questionnaires, observations and impressions, and case histories of the institutions. Goodlad presents the conclusions as "postulates" or objectives for the renewal of teacher education. Of the 19 listed in the book, nine appear to have a direct bearing on some aspect of the initial teacher preparation curriculum. Those are:

Postulate Four: There must exist a clearly identifiable group of academic and clinical faculty members for whom teacher education is the top priority. The group must be responsible and accountable for selecting students and mentoring their progress, planning and maintaining the full scope and sequence of the curriculum, continuously evaluating and improving programs, and facilitating the entry of graduates into teaching careers.

Postulate Eight: Programs for the education of educators must provide extensive opportunities for future teachers to move beyond being students of organized knowledge to become teachers who inquire into both knowledge and its teaching.

Postulate Ten: Programs for the education of educators must be characterized in all respects by the conditions for learning that

82

future teachers are to establish in their own schools and class-rooms.

Postulate Eleven: Programs for the education of educators must be conducted in such a way that future teachers inquire into the nature of teaching and schooling and that they will do so as a natural aspect of their careers.

Postulate Twelve: Programs for the education of educators must involve future teachers in the issues and dilemmas that emerge out of the never-ending tensions between the rights and interests of individual parents and social-interest groups, on one hand, and the role of schools in transcending parochialism, on the other.

Postulate Thirteen: Programs for the education of educators must be infused with understanding of and commitment to the moral obligation of teachers to ensure equitable access to and engagement in the best possible K-12 education for all children.

Postulate Fourteen: Programs for the education of educators must involve future teachers not only in understanding schools as they are, but also the alternatives, the assumptions underlying alternatives, and how to effect needed changes in school organization, pupil grouping, curriculum, and more.

Postulate Fifteen: Programs for the education of educators must ensure for each candidate the availability of a wide array of laboratory settings for observation, hands-on experiences, and exemplary schools for internships and residencies. They must admit no more students to their programs than can be ensured these quality experiences.

Postulate Sixteen: Programs for the education of educators must engage future teachers in the problems and dilemmas arising out of the inevitable conflicts and incongruities between what works or is accepted in practice and the research and theory supporting other options.

NNER members must make a dual commitment to the process of simultaneous renewal of initial teacher preparation and the improvement of schools in which their graduates will teach. The member institutions are located in regions across the country and work in networks in which one or more colleges or universities engage in the process of "developing an organic relationship with partner schools" (Goodlad 1994, p. 636) and commit to the mission, agenda, and process of renewal advocated in the 19 postulates.

29. The Teacher Testing Movement

By the 1990s, competency-based assessment of beginning teachers increasingly influenced the preparation curriculum. Results of such tests were being used to control entrance into and exit out of teacher preparation programs and also licensure or certification. If this trend continues, teacher preparation may be driven by tests and testing companies.

One of the most visible contributors to this movement is the Educational Testing Service (ETS), which has developed a series of competency-based teacher tests, *The Praxis Series: Professional Assessments for Beginning Teachers* (Dwyer and Villegas 1992). The *Praxis Series* consists of three parts: *Praxis I* measures basic academic skills; *Praxis II* measures knowledge of subject matter and pedagogy; and *Praxis III* evaluates teaching skill. The first two parts of the *Praxis Series* are essentially the same as the components of the *National Teachers Exam* used in at least 33 states for evaluation of preservice teacher general knowledge, subject matter, and pedagogical knowledge. However, *Praxis III* is a system for assessing the skills of preservice and beginning teachers in their own classroom settings, using three assessment methods: direct observation of classroom practice, review of written documentation prepared by the teacher, and semi-structured interviews. The assessment strategy groups teaching tasks into four broad areas or domains with specific performance criteria defined and explained for each area. These domains and their associated performance criteria are:

1. Organizing content knowledge for student learning:
   a. becoming familiar with relevant aspects of students' background knowledge and experiences;

b. articulating clear learning goals for the lesson that are appropriate for students;

c. demonstrating an understanding of the connections between content that was learned previously, the current content, and the content that remains to be learned in the future;

d. creating or selecting teaching methods, learning activities, and instructional materials or other resources that are appropriate for students and that are aligned with the goals of the lesson; and

e. creating or selecting evaluation strategies that are appropriate for students and that are aligned with the goals of the lesson.

2. Creating an environment for student learning:
   a. creating a climate that promotes fairness;
   b. establishing and maintaining rapport with students;
   c. communicating challenging learning expectations to each student;
   d. establishing and maintaining consistent standards of classroom behavior; and
   e. making the physical environment as safe and conducive to learning as possible.

3. Teaching for student learning:
   a. making learning goals and instructional procedures clear;
   b. making content comprehensible to students;
   c. encouraging students to extend their thinking;
   d. monitoring students' understanding of content through a variety of means, providing feedback to students to assist learning, and adjusting learning activities as the situation demands; and
   e. using instructional time effectively.

4. Teacher professionalism:
   a. reflecting on the extent to which learning goals were met;
   b. demonstrating a sense of efficacy;

c. building professional relationships with colleagues to share teaching insights and to coordinate learning activities for students; and

d. communicating with parents or guardians about student learning (ETS 1994).

The four domains and the performance criteria are considered by ETS to be "interrelated aspects or facets of a complex set of actions and cognitions called 'teaching', not . . . independent constructs or 'pieces' of teaching" (Dwyer and Villegas 1994). Furthermore, they are affected by circumstances unique to each teaching situation. Thus individual, developmental, and cultural differences in the student population, as well as subject matter differences, are considered in the assessment process.

Teacher education institutions that choose to adopt the *Praxis III* program receive training through *Pathwise,* an observation-based teacher support program developed by ETS. This training offers "an efficient, nationally validated method of standardizing student teaching observation. The system can also be used in guiding the development of teacher training curriculum" (ETS 1994).

Observations

Having presented more than two dozen proposals intended to improve teacher preparation, we now attempt a brief analysis of them. This task is difficult, because each proposal is presented in a unique format and style and varies in what it addresses, its comprehensiveness and length, and its clarity. However, our analysis is aided by an earlier, more comprehensive analysis that looked at many of the same pre-1987 proposals (Cruickshank and Troyer 1991).

Many of the proposals seem to have been in response to scientific, social, and economic challenges that America has faced in the past four decades. Such circumstances led to the conclusion that schools were failing and, relatedly, that teachers and teaching were below par. Other proposals resulted from forays into education and teacher education by university leaders, researchers and theoreticians, journalists, visionaries, teacher and teacher education organizations, and philosophic foundations. Many of these latter proposals also were reactions to national concerns.

The Teacher's Role. It could be argued that a professional program should be designed to prepare teachers who can assume a specific role or roles in K-12 schools (Cruickshank 1971). In a few cases, the reform proposals seem to suggest what these roles are, though in most cases they are not stated explicitly. The 10 roles for teachers that seem to come from these reform proposals are:

1. *A competent teacher.* Such teachers know what good or effective K-12 practitioners do and they are able to demonstrate those abilities.
2. *A student of teaching.* These teachers are reflective; that is, they give careful consideration to the act of teaching and its effects.
3. *A community builder.* These practitioners are humane persons who enhance the self-image of students and members of the community.
4. *An artist.* Such teachers know who they are, what they are like, and how they can use their unique talent to enhance student learning.
5. *A concerned teacher.* Such practitioners are more concerned with the needs of students and less concerned with their own needs.
6. *An actor.* These teachers understand the role of "effective classroom practitioner" and have acquired the abilities to perform it.
7. *A problem solver/decision maker.* Such teachers are able to resolve problems and make decisions in such a way that benefits accrue to all parties.
8. *An enlightened teacher.* Such practitioners are well-educated and are concerned primarily with helping students to become well-educated.
9. *A culturally responsible teacher.* These teachers are ready and able to work with diverse students in diverse communities.

10. *An inquiring teacher*. Such teachers engage in inquiry related to teaching and learning.

The Curriculum. Not all of the proposals present an overview of what should be in the preparation curriculum. Those that do generally adhere to the idea of three components of the teacher education curriculum, consisting of general studies, content studies, and professional education, including pedagogy and on- and off-campus laboratory and clinical experiences.

When general studies are addressed, with one exception (Smith et al. 1980), the argument is that they are critical, that they need improvement, and that more of them should be required.

Content studies uniformly are endorsed when they are mentioned. However, one issue is whether academic professors who teach such courses can shape them for prospective teachers.

One proposal (Howsam et al. 1976) calls for the introduction of another curriculum component, termed *education in the undergirding disciplines*. In that component, preservice teachers would study those subjects to which educators regularly look for professional advice and guidance, such as psychology and sociology.

Without question, the professional component is addressed most often in these reform proposals. Among the more prominent suggestions are that preservice teachers should:

1. Study the foundations of education. However, these foundational studies are in need of refocus and redirection.
2. Be knowledgeable about child development.
3. Know, understand, and accept themselves.
4. Be prepared to be humane, that is, sensitive and caring advocates for all young people.
5. Be experienced with cultures other than their own.
6. Be knowledgeable about learning theory.
7. Be skillful in observation and diagnostic techniques.
8. Be skillful in methods of observation and inquiry so that they themselves can study teaching and learning.
9. Be able to promote a positive classroom learning environment.

10. Be skillful in the elements of the act of teaching, that is, finding out about students, planning suitable instruction, using variety in facilitating learning, assessment, and management.

11. Be able to use teacher attributes and teaching behaviors found to be associated with student learning and satisfaction.

12. Be able to analyze classroom situations and to use related knowledge to understand, and resolve attendant issues and problems.

13. Be reflective and introspective with regard to their teaching and its influence and effects.

14. Be skillful in the regular techniques of teaching, including presenting and questioning.

15. Be knowledgeable about the organized teaching profession and capable of making thoughtful professional judgments.

16. Be able to demonstrate in on- and off-campus experiences all of the above and that, when they teach, learners learn and are satisfied.

Considerable disagreement continues to exist between those who believe that teachers can be prepared adequately within four years and those who wish to devote the undergraduate curriculum to general and content studies and move professional education to the graduate level. Of course, some argue that teachers need only to be well-educated generally and know their subject.

Another unresolved issue relates to where teachers should be prepared. Some believe that teacher preparation should be conducted mostly on campus with heavy reliance on *campus-based* laboratory and clinical kinds of experiences. Others argue that teaching can be learned only where it naturally occurs.

Perhaps the most bewildering observation resulting from perusing the various reform proposals is that the authors seem to be almost oblivious of each other's work. Rarely does one acknowledge or refer to another. The reason for this curious behavior is uncertain and troublesome, particularly when each seems to draw on or repeat earlier themes and ideas.

Recommendations

Over the years, a number of persons have given considerable time and serious thought to preparing teachers. However, few have addressed the preparation curriculum *per se*. And because little long-term notice is given to alternative ideas for improved teacher preparation, these ideas soon are shelved and forgotten. In fact, some ideas are touted as new when they are resurrections of old ideas.

The issues or matters of debate regarding the teacher preparation curriculum should be isolated, studied, and debated. Some of these issues are:

- Who should be in charge and responsible for teacher preparation and its curriculum?
- What should constitute the curriculum for initial teacher preparation?
- What should be the balance of various studies and experiences?
- Where should teacher preparation occur?
- How much teacher preparation is necessary?
- Should teacher preparation be a responsibility of the entire university?
- Should teacher preparation be an undergraduate experience, a graduate experience, or both?
- What should be the role of the teacher in K-12 schools?

References

AACTE Committee on Performance-Based Teacher Education. *Achieving the Potential of Performance-Based Teacher Education: Recommendations*. Washington, D.C.: American Association of Colleges for Teacher Education, February 1974.

Adler, M. *The Paideia Proposal: An Educational Manifesto*. New York: Macmillan, 1982.

Arciniega, T. "Planning and Organizational Issues Involved in Operationalizing the Multicultural Educational Standard." Paper presented at the American Association of Colleges for Teacher

Education Leadership Training Institute on Multicultural Education in Washington, D.C., December 1977.

Association of Teacher Educators. *Restructuring the Education of Teachers: The 21st Century.* Reston, Va., 1991.

Bainer, D.L. "Perceived Problems of Elementary Teachers Related to Grade Level, Teaching Experience, and Student Background." Doctoral dissertation, Ohio State University, 1986.

Banks, J.A. "A Response to Philip Freedman." *Phi Delta Kappan* 58 (May 1977): 695-97.

Borich, G. "Implications for Developing Teacher Competencies from Process-Product Research." *Journal of Teacher Education* 30, no. 1 (1979): 77-86.

Boyer, E. *High School: A Report on Secondary Education in America.* New York: Harper & Row, 1983.

Brophy, J. "Teacher Behavior and Its Effects." *Journal of Educational Psychology* 71, no. 6 (1979): 733-50.

Buckley, W.F. "Firing Line: The Paideia Proposal." Transcript. Public Broadcasting Network, 7 November 1982.

Carnegie Council on Adolescent Development. *Turning Points: Preparing American Youth for the 21st Century.* Washington, D.C., 1989.

Carnegie Task Force on Teaching as a Profession. *A Nation Prepared: Teachers for the 21st Century.* New York: Carnegie Forum on Education and the Economy, 1986.

Combs, A. "Teacher Education: The Person in the Process." *Educational Leadership* 35 (1978): 558-61.

Combs, A.; Blume, R.; Newman, R.; and Wass, H. *The Professional Education of Teachers.* Boston: Allyn and Bacon, 1974.

Commission on Multicultural Education. *Directory: Multicultural Education Programs in Teacher Education Institutions in the United States.* Washington, D.C.: American Association of Colleges for Teacher Education, 1978.

Conant, J. *The Education of American Teachers.* New York: McGraw-Hill, 1963.

Cruickshank, D.R. *The Inner-City Simulation Laboratory.* Chicago: Science Research Associates, 1969.

Cruickshank, D.R. *Blueprints for Teacher Education: A Review of Phase II Proposals for the USOE Comprehensive Elementary Teacher Education (CETEM) Program.* Washington, D.C.: U.S. Department of Health, Education and Welfare, 1970. ERIC Document Reproduction Service No. ED 013 371.

Cruickshank, D.R. "Conceptualizing a Process for Teacher Education Curriculum Development." *Journal of Teacher Education* 22, no. 1 (1971): 73-82.

Cruickshank, D.R. "Synthesis of Selected Research on Teacher Effects." *Journal of Teacher Education* 27, no. 1 (1976): 57-60.

Cruickshank, D.R. *Research that Informs Teachers and Teacher Educators.* Bloomington, Ind.: Phi Delta Kappa Educational Foundation, 1990.

Cruickshank, D.R.; Applegate, J.; Holton, J.; Mager, J.; Myers, B.; Novak, C.; and Tracey, K. *Teaching Is Tough.* Englewood Cliffs, N.J.: Prentice-Hall, 1980.

Cruickshank, D.R., and Broadbent, F. *The Simulation and Analysis of Problems of Beginning Teachers.* Research Project No. 5-0789. Washington, D.C.: U.S. Government Printing Office, 1968. ERIC Document Reproduction Service No. ED 024 637.

Cruickshank, D.R.; Broadbent, F.; and Bubb, R. *The Teaching Problems Laboratory.* Chicago: Science Research Associates, 1967.

Cruickshank, D.R.; Holton, J.; Fay, D.; Williams, J.; Kennedy, J.; Myers, B.; and Hough, B. *Reflective Teaching.* Bloomington, Ind.: Phi Delta Kappa, 1980, 1991.

Cruickshank, D.R.; Kennedy, J.; Leonard, J.; and Thurman, R. *Perceived Problems of Teachers in Schools Serving Rural Disadvantaged Populations: A Comparison with Problems Reported by Inner-City Teachers.* NDEA National Institute for Advanced Study of Disadvantaged Youth Occasional Paper No. 5. Washington, D.C.: American Association of Colleges for Teacher Education, 1968. ERIC Document Reproduction Service No. 027 986.

Cruickshank, D.R.; Kennedy, J.; and Myers, B. "Perceived Problems of Secondary School Teachers." *Journal of Educational Research* 68 (1974): 154-59.

Cruickshank, D.R., and Leonard, J. *The Identification and Analysis of Perceived Problems of Teachers in Inner-City Schools.* NDEA National Institute for Advanced Study in Teaching Disadvantaged Youth Occasional Paper No. 1. Washington, D.C.: American Association of Colleges for Teacher Education, 1967. ERIC Document Reproduction Service No. 026 335.

Cruickshank, D.R., and Troyer, M. "What Reformers Would Have Us Do." *Midwestern Educational Researcher* 4, no. 1 (1991): 5-8.

Darling-Hammond, L. "Who Will Speak for the Children? How 'Teach for America' Hurts Urban Schools and Students." *Phi Delta Kappan* 76 (September 1994): 21-34.

Dodl, N.; Elfner, E.; Becker, J.; Halstead, J.; Jung, H.; Nelson, P.; Purinton, S.; and Wegele, P. *Florida Catalog of Teacher Competencies.* Tallahassee: Florida State University, 1972.

Doyle, W. "Research on Teaching in Classroom Environments." Paper presented at the National Invitational Conference Exploring Issues in Teacher Education: Questions for Future Research, in Austin, Texas, January 1979.

Doyle, W. "Academic Work." *Review of Educational Research* 53, no. 2 (1983): 159-99.

Dunkin, M., and Biddle, B. *A Study of Teaching.* New York: Holt, Rinehart and Winston, 1974.

Dwyer, C.A., and Villegas, A.M. *The Praxis Series: Professional Assessments for Beginning Teachers.* Princeton, N.J.: Educational Testing Service, 1992.

Dwyer, C.A., and Villegas, A.M. *Praxis III: Classroom Performance Assessments.* Princeton, N.J.: Educational Testing Service, 1994.

Educational Testing Service (ETS). *Praxis III: Classroom Performance Assessments, Assessment Criteria.* Princeton, N.J.: Educational Testing Service, September 1994.

Fuller, F. "Concerns of Teachers: A Developmental Conceptualization." *American Educational Research Journal* 6 (1969): 207-26.

Fuller, F. "A Conceptual Framework for a Personalized Teacher Education Program." *Theory Into Practice* 13, no. 2 (1974): 112-22.

Fuller, F., and Bown, O. "Becoming a Teacher." In *Teacher Education,* edited by K. Ryan. Chicago: University of Chicago Press, 1975.

Gage, N.L. "Paradigms for Research on Teaching." In *Handbook of Research on Teaching,* edited by N.L. Gage. Chicago: Rand McNally, 1963.

Gage, N.L. *The Scientific Basis of the Art of Teaching.* New York: Teachers College Press, 1978.

Gideonse, H.D. "The Necessary Revolution in Teacher Education." *Phi Delta Kappan* 64 (September 1982): 15-18.

Good, T. "Classroom Research: A Decade of Progress." Paper presented at the meeting of the American Educational Research Association in Montreal, 1983.

Good, T., and McCaslin, M.M. "Teacher Effectiveness." In *Encyclopedia of Educational Research,* 6th ed., edited by M. Alkin. New York: Macmillan, 1992.

Goodlad, J. *Teachers for Our Nation's Schools.* San Francisco: Jossey-Bass, 1990.

Goodlad, J. "The National Network for Educational Renewal." *Phi Delta Kappan* 75 (April 1994): 632-38.

Griffin, G. "Using Research in Preservice Teacher Education." Paper presented for the Improving Preservice Teacher Education Project in Detroit, 1983.

Hidalgo, H. "No One Model American." *Journal of Teacher Education* 24, no. 4 (1973): 254-65.

Holmes Group. *Tomorrow's Teachers: A Report of the Holmes Group.* East Lansing, Mich., 1986.

Holmes Group. *Tomorrow's Schools of Education.* East Lansing: Michigan State University, 1995.

Howsam, R.B.; Corrigan, D.; Denemark, G.; and Nash, R. *Educating a Profession.* Washington, D.C.: American Association of Colleges for Teacher Education, 1976.

Hunter, W., ed. *Multicultural Education Through Competency-Based Teacher Education.* Washington, D.C.: American Association of Colleges for Teacher Education, 1974.

LaGrone, H. *A Proposal for the Revision of the Pre-Service Professional Component of Teacher Education.* Washington, D.C.: American Association of Colleges for Teacher Education, 1964.

McDonald, F.J. "The National Commission on Performance-Based Education." *Phi Delta Kappan* 55 (January 1974): 296-98.

Medley, D. *Teacher Competence and Teacher Effectiveness.* Washington, D.C.: American Association of Colleges for Teacher Education, 1977.

Murray, F., and Fallon, D. *The Reform of Teacher Education for the 21st Century: Project 30 One Year Report.* New York: Carnegie Foundation for the Advancement of Teaching, 1989. ERIC Document Reproduction Service No. 355 178.

National Advisory Council on Education Professions Development. *Teacher Corps: Past or Prologue.* Washington, D.C., 1975.

National Commission on Excellence in Education. *A Nation at Risk: The Imperative for Educational Reform.* Washington, D.C.: U.S. Department of Education, 1983.

National Commission for Excellence in Teacher Education. *A Call for Change in Teacher Education.* Washington, D.C.: American Association of Colleges for Teacher Education, 1985.

National Council for Accreditation of Teacher Education. *Standards for the Accreditation of Teacher Education.* Washington, D.C., 1982.

National Council for Accreditation of Teacher Education. *Standards for the Accreditation of Teacher Education.* Washington, D.C., 1990.

National Council for Accreditation of Teacher Education. *Standards for the Accreditation of Teacher Education.* Washington, D.C., 1995.

National Education Association. *Excellence in Our Schools: Teacher Education, An Action Plan.* Washington, D.C., 1982.

Olson, P.; Freeman, L.; and Bowman, J., eds. *Education for 1984 and After.* Lincoln: University of Nebraska, 1972.

Olson, P.; Freeman, L.; Bowman, J.; and Pieper, J. *The University Can't Train Teachers.* Lincoln: University of Nebraska Curriculum Development Center, 1972.

Pennsylvania Department of Education. *Generic Teaching Competencies.* Harrisburg, 1973.

Philosophy of Education Society. "Standards for Academic and Professional Instruction in Philosophy of Education." *Educational Theory* 30 (1980): 265-68.

Porter, A.C., and Brophy, J. "A Synthesis of Research on Good Teaching: Insights from the Work of the Institute for Research on Teaching." *Educational Leadership* 45, no. 8 (1988): 74-85.

Powell, M. "Research on Teaching." *Educational Forum* 43, no. 1 (1978): 27-37.

Renaissance Group. *Educating the New American Student.* Cedar Falls, Iowa, 1993.

Rosenshine, B. *Teaching Behaviors and Student Achievement.* International Association for the Evaluation of Educational Achievement IEA Studies No. 1. National Foundation for Educational Research in England and Wales, 1971.

Rosenshine, B., and Furst, N. "Research on Teacher Performance Criteria." In *Research in Teacher Education,* edited by B.O. Smith. Englewood Cliffs, N.J.: Prentice-Hall, 1971.

Scannell, D.; Corrigan, D.; Denemark, G.; Dieterle, L.; Egbert, R.; and Nielson, R. *Educating a Profession: Profile of a Beginning Teacher.* Washington, D.C.: American Association of Colleges for Teacher Education, 1983.

Schorr, J. "Class Action: What Clinton's National Service Program Could Learn from 'Teach for America'." *Phi Delta Kappan* 75 (November 1993): 315-18.

Silberman, C.E. *Crisis in the Classroom: The Remaking of American Education.* New York: Random House, 1970.

Smith, B.O.; Cohen, S.; and Pearl. A. *Teachers for the Real World.* Washington, D.C.: American Association of Colleges for Teacher Education, 1969.

Smith, B.O.; Silverman, S.; Borg, J.; and Fry, B. *A Design for a School of Pedagogy.* Washington, D.C.: U.S. Department of Education, 1980.

Soar, R.S., and Soar, R.M. "An Attempt to Identify Measures of Teacher Effectiveness from Four Studies." *Journal of Teacher Education* 27, no. 3 (1976): 261-67.

Stallings, J. "Implications from the Research on Teaching for Teacher Preparation." Paper presented at the Improving Preservice Teacher Education Project in Detroit, 1983.

Study Commission on Undergraduate Education and the Education of Teachers. *Teacher Education in the United States: The Responsibility Gap.* Lincoln: University of Nebraska Press, 1976.

Travers, R. "Empirically Based Teacher Education." *Educational Forum* 39 (1975): 417-34.

Travers, R., and Dillon, J. *The Making of a Teacher.* New York: Macmillan, 1975.

Verduin, J.R. *Conceptual Models in Teacher Education.* Washington, D.C.: American Association of Colleges for Teacher Education, 1967.

Walberg, H.J. "Synthesis of Research on Teaching." In *Handbook of Research on Teaching*, 3rd ed., edited by M.C. Wittrock. New York: Macmillan, 1986.

Related Readings

Amidon, E., and Flanders, N. *The Role of the Teacher in the Classroom: A Manual for Understanding and Improving Teachers' Classroom Behavior.* Minneapolis: Paul S. Amidon & Associates, 1963.

Armaline, W. "A Philosophical Analysis of Teacher Clarity." Doctoral dissertation, Ohio State University, 1985.

Bellack, A., and Davity, J. *The Language of the Classroom.* U.S. Department of Health, Education and Welfare Cooperative Research Project No. 1497. New York: Columbia University, Teachers College, Institute of Psychological Research, 1963.

Broudy, H. *The Real World of Public Schools.* New York: Harcourt Brace Jovanovich, 1972.

Broudy, H.; Smith, B.; and Burnett, J. *Democracy and Excellence in American Secondary Education.* Chicago: Rand McNally, 1964.

Bruner, J. *The Process of Education.* Cambridge, Mass.: Harvard University Press, 1962.

Bush, A. "An Empirical Exploration of Teacher Clarity." Doctoral dissertation, Ohio State University, 1976.

Bush, A.; Kennedy, J.; and Cruickshank, D. "An Empirical Investigation of Teacher Clarity." *Journal of Teacher Education* 28 (1977): 53-58.

Corrigan, D. "American Association of Colleges for Teacher Education, National Education Association Action Plan: Outlines for Reform." *AACTE Briefs* 3, no. 7 (1982): 1-3.

Cruickshank, D.R.; Kennedy, J.; Bush, A.; and Myers, B. "Clear Teaching: What Is It?" *British Journal of Teacher Education* 5 (1979): 27-33.

Emmer, E.; Evertson, C.; and Anderson, L. "Effective Management at the Beginning of the School Year." *Elementary School Journal* 80 (1980): 219-31.

Evertson, C., and Anderson, L. "Beginning School." *Educational Horizons* 57 (1979): 164-68.

Galloway, C. "An Exploratory Study of Observational Procedures for Determining Teacher Non-Verbal Communication." Doctoral dissertation, University of Florida, 1962.

Getzels, J., and Thelen, H. "The Classroom Group as a Unique Social System." In *The Fifty-Sixth Yearbook of the National Society for the Study of Education, Part II,* edited by R. Preston. Chicago: University of Chicago Press, 1957.

Gutek, G.L. *An Historical Introduction to American Education.* New York: Thomas Y. Crowell, Harper & Row, 1970.

Hall, E. *The Silent Language.* New York: Doubleday, 1959.

Hamilton, S. "An Investigation of Teacher Clarity Among Selected Student Teachers Involved in a National Competition." Doctoral dissertation, Ohio State University, 1988.

Heath, R., and Nielson, M. "The Research Basis for Performance-Based Teacher Education." *Review of Educational Research* 44 (1972): 463-84.

Hickey, A., and Newton, J. *The Logical Basis of Teaching: I. The Effect of Subconcept Sequence on Learning.* Newburyport, Mass.: ENTELEK, 1964.

Hines, C. "A Further Investigation of Teacher Clarity: The Observation of Teacher Clarity and the Relationship Between Clarity and Student Achievement and Satisfaction." Doctoral dissertation, Ohio State University, 1981.

Hines, C.; Kennedy, J.; and Cruickshank, D. "Teacher Clarity and Its Relationship to Student Achievement and Satisfaction." *American Research Journal* 22 (1985): 87-99.

Houston, R. *Developing Instructional Modules.* Houston: University of Houston College of Education, 1972.

Jenkins, D. "Characteristics and Functions of Leadership in Instructional Groups." In *The Fifty-Ninth Yearbook of the National Society for the Study of Education, Part II,* edited by G. Jenson. Chicago: University of Chicago Press, 1960.

Joyce, B., and Weil, M. *Models of Teaching.* Englewood Cliffs, N.J.: Prentice-Hall, 1972.

Kennedy, J.; Cruickshank, D.; Bush, A.; and Myers, B. "Additional Investigation into the Nature of Teacher Clarity." *Journal of Educational Research* 72 (1978): 3-10.

Kounin, J. *Discipline and Group Management in Classrooms.* New York: Holt, Rinehart and Winston, 1970.

Larsen, P. "Teacher Clarity as a Critical Variable in the Training and Evaluation of Mathematics Teachers, and as a Variable Associated with Student Achievement." Doctoral dissertation, Ohio State University, 1985.

Lumsdaine, A. "Educational Technology, Programmed Learning, and Instructional Science." In *The Sixty-Third Yearbook of the National Society for the Study of Education, Part I.* Chicago: University of Chicago Press, 1964.

Maccia, E.; Maccia, G.; and Jewett, R. *Construction of Educational Theory Models.* U.S. Office of Education Cooperative Research Project No. 1932. Columbus: Ohio State University, 1963.

Mager, R. *Preparing Objectives for Programmed Instruction.* San Francisco: Fearon, 1962.

Metcalf, K. "An Investigation of the Efficacy of a Research-Based Regimen of Skill Development on the Instructional Clarity of Preservice Teachers." Doctoral dissertation, Ohio State University, 1989.

Metcalf, K., and Cruickshank, D. "Can Teachers Be Trained to Be More Clear?" *Journal of Educational Research* 85, no. 2 (1991): 107.

Monroe, W.S. *Teaching Learning Theory and Teacher Education.* Urbana: University of Illinois Press, 1952.

Murray, Frank B. "Holmes Group Pursues Reform Agenda." *The School Administrator* 2 (1987): 29-34.

National Center for Research in Vocational Education. *Handbook for the Development of Professional Vocational Teacher Education Modules.* Columbus: Ohio State University, 1973.

Rosenshine, B., and Berliner, D. "Academic Engaged Time." *British Journal of Teacher Education* 4 (1978): 3-16.

Scheffler, I. "University Scholarship and the Education of Teachers." *Teachers College Record* 70 (1968): 1-12.

Smith, B.O., and Ennis, H. *Language and Concepts in Education.* Chicago: Rand McNally, 1961.

Smith, B.O., and Meuz, M. *A Study of the Logic of Teaching.* U.S. Department of Health, Education and Welfare Cooperative Research Project No. 235. Urbana: University of Illinois, 1962.

Suchman, J. *The Elementary School Training Program in Scientific Inquiry.* U.S. Office of Education Title VII Cooperative Research Project No. 216. Champaign-Urbana: University of Illinois, 1964.

Taba, H.; Levine, S.; and Elzey, F. *Thinking in Elementary School Children.* U.S. Office of Education Cooperative Research Project No. 1574. San Francisco: San Francisco State College, 1964.

Williams, J. "The Short Term Stability of Teacher Clarity." Doctoral dissertation, Ohio State University, 1983.

Withall, J. "The Development of a Technique for the Measurement of Social Emotional Climate in Classrooms." *Journal of Experimental Education* 17 (1949): 347.

Woodruff, A. "The Use of Concepts in Teaching." *Journal of Teacher Education* 15 (1964): 81-99.

Woodruff, A. "The Nature and Elements of the Cognitive Approach to Instruction." *Education* 34 (May 1964): 3-9.

Chapter 3
*S*IX PROMISING APPROACHES TO TEACHER EDUCATION

It is one thing to decide *what* to teach prospective teachers. It is quite another thing to know *how* to teach it. Fortunately, the vast majority of faculty in colleges of education have benefited from their own professional preparation as K-12 teachers. They specifically studied teaching and learning and engaged in extensive supervised teaching practice. Furthermore, to gain state eligibility to become teacher educators, most college faculty had to teach in K-12 schools for at least three years. Thus teacher educators should know both what and how to teach. Unfortunately, many still can be heard to lament, "Why don't I teach as well as I know how?"

Among the factors contributing to the success of teachers at any level is their ability to use a variety of instructional alternatives. Indeed, most states require that those who prepare teachers use instructional variety. For example, the National Association of State Directors of Teacher Education and Certification included in its 1981 *Standards* the requirement that "The institution shall provide evidence that its faculty uses a variety of instructional procedures" (p. 10).

There are at least 29 instructional alternatives that teacher educators can use (Cruickshank, Bainer, and Metcalf 1995). However, a few have special value in teacher preparation. They include cases, microteaching, minicourses, protocols, reflective teaching, and simulations.

Each of these is a form of on-campus laboratory experience. Each offers a potentially valuable addition to, or replacement for, current practice in teacher preparation. And each provides students the opportunity to apply knowledge to realistic situations while also allowing greater reflection and analysis of the experience. Thus they offer more reasonable, and likely more effective, approaches than do either didactic coursework or extensive field experiences (Berliner 1985; Evertson 1990; Metcalf 1994). These alternatives frequently are ignored or overlooked, perhaps because they require considerable time to prepare and implement or because they require teacher educators to assume a role different from that with which they are familiar.

Case Studies

A case study is a carefully recorded story or account of something that actually happened. However, in some instances a useful case study for teacher preparation may be a composite of fact and fiction.

Cases have long been developed for use in law, medicine, and business. Having noted their successful use in the Harvard Business School and elsewhere, professors of educational administration began in the 1950s and 1960s to develop numerous instructional cases that could be used in the preparation of school administrative personnel. Shortly thereafter, teacher educators wrote a great many, mostly brief, cases that were made available commercially. A resurgence of teacher educator interest in case studies or case method has occurred since the mid-1980s (Harrington 1991).

Lawrence (1953) describes a good case as:

> a vehicle by which a chunk of reality is brought into the classroom to be worked over by the class and the instructor. A good case keeps the class discussion grounded upon some of the stubborn facts that must be faced up to in real life situations . . . it is the record of complex situations that must be literally pulled apart and put together again before the situations can be understood. (p. 215)

Instructors in teacher education may have available two kinds of cases. One is a rich, extended account or description of a student teaching experience. The case would include daily, perhaps hourly detail of what happened, when, where, and how. Because of the breadth of coverage this case provides, it can be introduced and discussed at the first class session and then looked at again when it is appropriate to parallel experiences the students are having at their workplaces.

Another kind of case is more brief and focused. It might be a description of a single event or circumstance that occurred within the student teaching experience. Such cases have great potential value but usually are of specific and short-lived interest.

Cases can be used to achieve two outcomes. The first is understanding. The case can be used to help prospective student teachers gain a glimpse of the realities they will be facing. It can be used to help them better understand specific aspects of that reality, such as relationships, responsibilities, communication, classroom climate, motivation, and so forth. This understanding is enhanced as the university instructor guides the students through analysis of the case.

In addition to fostering greater understanding, cases also can be used to foster problem solving. When using this kind of case, the instructor can either have students analyze the event and its outcome or ask them what they would have done in the same situation. Sykes and Bird (1992) note that when students are confronted with cases that demonstrate problems of teaching, they have the opportunity to examine their own beliefs, assumptions, and biases.

Although the case method appears to have the potential to enhance teacher preparation, it has not been studied extensively, and the studies that have been done have shown mixed results. Kleinfeld (1991) reports the case method to be significantly more effective than "guided discussion" in promoting preservice teachers' ability to analyze educational problems. However, the study found no significant differences in the subjects' attitudes toward the two instructional methods or their views of the teacher as a professional. Gliessman, Geillo, and Archer (1989) find the case method, when used in combination with other instructional methods (for example, peer teaching or lectures) to enable preservice teachers to interpret educational problems.

However, Butler (1966) reports that while participants respond positively to case method instruction, the method demonstrates no significant differences in student learning of the target concepts. And both Argyris (1980) and Leone (1989), after comparing case-based teaching with other instructional alternatives, conclude that a case-based curriculum is an inefficient way to convey "codified knowledge" useful to a complex practice; that single, vivid cases do not help students see underlying issues and develop useful and generalizable principles; and that case discussions lack the impact of experiential or on-the-job learning. Sykes and Bird's (1992) review of similar research raises questions about the effectiveness of the case method.

Ideally, the case method can have the following advantages:

1. It provides a rich and realistic insight into the real world of teaching.
2. It permits participants to see teaching, classroom, and school situations as complex.
3. It causes participants to engage in analysis or problem solving.
4. It causes participants to draw from and apply related theoretical knowledge.

The case method also can have the following disadvantages:

1. Too few quality cases exist to permit significant study of professional education and pedagogy.
2. Cases often are unclear and may lack sufficient information to permit thoughtful analysis and decision making.
3. The use of cases demands a great deal of time.
4. In order for the case method to work, instructors must be skillful in using discovery learning and discussion, be able to suspend their own judgment and bias, and have significant knowledge to assist participants in analyzing and understanding the case situations.

Microteaching

Microteaching was designed to promote the use of specific teaching abilities that are thought to contribute to effective teaching (Allen and Ryan 1969). In this method, preservice teachers 1) read about one of the abilities, such as "use of examples"; 2) prepare and teach a three- to five-minute lesson, which is videotaped and in which they demonstrate the ability, either to a small group of school-aged learners or to peers; and 3) view the videotape and receive feedback from a university instructor regarding their performance. Then they either prepare and teach another lesson to improve their use of that ability or repeat the process with a different ability. After several abilities have been mastered, participants prepare and teach a longer lesson (usually 20 minutes) in which several abilities are demonstrated in concert.

McDonald, one of the originators of microteaching, soon became critical of the excessive attention given to the original teaching skills.

> Unfortunately, the concept of technical skills of teaching has been overly promoted and inaccurately described. They are not basic or essential because there is no data to show that a teacher who uses them produces more effective learning. They may have an important effect on learning but that remains to be shown. (1973, p. 55)

There are teaching abilities or behaviors that are strongly and consistently associated with pupil academic gain and satisfaction (Cruickshank 1990). Some of these behaviors (for example, "direct instruction, group alerting, clarity, enthusiasm, and high expectations for pupil performance") have greater predictive validity than do the teaching skills originally used with microteaching. As a consequence, the skills taught through microteaching have increased in number and variety.

Microteaching is one of the most extensively used instructional methods in the teacher education curriculum. It reportedly is used in some variation by 91% of teacher education programs (McIntyre 1991). It also has been the subject of extensive research. However, MacLeod (1987) cautions that "despite an enormity of research endeavor, there are few definitive conclusions that can be drawn about the . . . effectiveness of microteaching" (p. 538).

Copeland (1975, 1977, 1982) and Copeland and Doyle (1973) have been associated with microteaching and its related research for some time. Copeland and others (for example, Winitsky and Arends 1991) report that preservice students can and do gain the target skills as a consequence of microteaching. Almost all the research supports this conclusion.

However, Copeland finds that these trained students are no more likely than others to use those skills later, during student teaching. Copeland (1975) determined that students' failure to use the skills during student teaching is not simply a matter of forgetting how to perform the skills. Rather, he determined that the key factor was the influence of the cooperating teachers.

Copeland (1982) also reports other research that finds that students who participate in microteaching show increased confidence in their teaching abilities and seem to have an increase in their overall level of self-esteem.

Among the major benefits attributed to microteaching are:

1. Microteaching is real teaching, as opposed to role-playing.
2. Microteaching reduces the complexity of the teaching act, allowing concentration on acquiring a specific skill.
3. Microteaching provides a relatively safe and controlled environment in which to practice.
4. Technical skills learned during microteaching can, with the proper reinforcement, result in their use in natural classrooms.
5. Microteaching may promote greater ability to think about, reflect on, and analyze teaching (Winitsky and Arends 1991).

However, microteaching does have several disadvantages. It requires considerable time and equipment, and there seldom is time for students to acquire more than one or two microteaching skills. In addition, the technical skills that are targeted in microteaching may not be those found to be most strongly associated with effective teaching.

When microteaching appeared on the teacher education scene, it was viewed as a way to provide a missing link between theory and practice. It would reduce the need for difficult-to-schedule teaching practice in schools. But most important, it was seen as a way to acquire important teaching abilities. In retrospect, it would seem that microteaching has more then met its original purposes and serves as an unusually promising instructional alternative in teacher education. It is well-accepted by students. It provides a much needed form of direct experience using a model of reality under controlled supervision. It can familiarize preservice teachers with desirable and effective teaching abilities or approaches. And given sufficient coaching and reinforcement, the attitudes and abilities learned in microteaching can transfer to natural classrooms.

Minicourses

Minicourses are short instructional (often self-instructional) courses intended to help teachers gain particular abilities, such as "effective questioning." Minicourses therefore are similar to microteaching and follow roughly the same pattern of activities. However, they were developed as packages to be used with practicing teachers, rather than with preservice teachers. Twenty minicourses were developed between 1967 and 1971 by Borg and his associates at the federally supported Far West Laboratory for Education Research and Development.

Participants in minicourses follow a carefully prescribed regimen. First, they choose a teaching skill to be mastered. Then they read about the skill and do related exercises on the concept. Afterward, participants watch a videotape or film in which the skill is demonstrated. Then they are shown a short film or videotape of teachers using that skill and are asked to identify when the demonstration teacher is using it effectively. Having acquired some understanding of the skill and having seen it modeled, participants then attempt to demonstrate proficiency in the skill by teaching a 10-minute lesson to about five K-12 students. This lesson is recorded, and participants later view the lesson to assess how well they did. The assessment is facilitated by use of prepared evaluation forms. Finally, participants replan and reteach the lesson, taking into account what they learned from their first performance (Perott 1987).

Research on minicourses has revealed consistent and positive effects with practicing teachers. Many studies found that the classroom behavior of teachers who had taken minicourses while they were students to be significantly more desirable than the behavior of teachers who had not (Borg 1972; 1975; Borg, Langer, and Wilson 1975; Borg and Stone 1974; Gall et al. 1972; Hofmeister and Stowikowski 1972; and Rector, Hull, and Mohan 1972). Moreover, the single study that examined the longevity of minicourse effects found that teachers who had taken minicourses used the desired behaviors in their classrooms significantly more often than did their untrained peers up to 39 months after completion of the minicourse (Borg 1972).

In contrast, the effects of minicourse participation on preservice teachers' classroom behavior are less consistent. Kallenbach and Ward (1974) report the classroom behavior of student teachers who had participated in minicourses to be more desirable than for untrained teachers, and the effects to be more significant when the cooperating teacher also was familiar with the desired behaviors. However, Borg, Kallenbach, Morris, and Friebel (1969) and Katz (1976) report minicourse preparation to result in no significant changes in student teacher classroom behavior.

The advantages of minicourses include:

1. The minicourse modules are designed around broad clusters of abilities and provide conceptual understanding of each target behavior.
2. The minicourse modules provide guided practice in acquiring the target behaviors.
3. They seem consistently effective in bringing about desirable classroom behavior with practicing teachers.

4. Practicing teachers who develop desirable behaviors through minicourse preparation are likely to continue to make use of these behaviors for an extended period.

The disadvantages of minicourses include:

1. The modules are detailed and specific. Thus the minicourse materials are less amenable for use in diverse settings.
2. Use of the modules is time-consuming, requiring participants to spend several sessions developing competence in each cluster.
3. Minicourse materials also are time-consuming and expensive to produce.

Minicourses may be more effective than either microteaching or protocols alone, because minicourses give attention to both developing conceptual understanding and promoting skilled performance. This effect is substantial and long-lasting, especially with inservice teachers. As with microteaching, the effects of minicourse preparation on student teacher's classroom performance is enhanced when the cooperating teacher reinforces the target behaviors. Certainly, the minicourse alternative holds promise for use in teacher preparation.

Protocol Materials

Protocol materials, the brainchild of Smith, Cohen, and Pearl (1969), were introduced to help preservice teachers become aware of and understand important aspects of their future life in schools and classrooms. Smith and his associates felt strongly that:

> Teachers fail because they have not been trained to calmly analyze new situations against a firm background of relevant theory. Typically they base their interpretations of behavior on intuition and common sense. . . . If the teacher is incapable of *understanding* classroom situations, the actions he takes will often increase his difficulties. (Smith, Cohen, and Pearl 1969, pp. 28-29)

Protocol materials consist of two parts, protocols and materials. A *protocol* is a record of some carefully selected, important, school-related event or concept. The record can be written or audio- or video-recorded. The *material* is an organized collection of related, relevant knowledge intended to help preservice teachers better understand the event or phenomenon depicted in the protocol. Thus, if a protocol or recording was made of cheating behavior, then all knowledge about that phenomenon would be identified, organized, and made available to persons exposed to the protocol. Having been exposed to the protocol and the materials, preservice teachers presumably would now be able to understand and react to the targeted classroom phenomenon more calmly, analytically, and intelligently (Cruickshank and Haefele 1987).

Approximately 140 sets of protocol materials have been developed. Events and concepts depicted include: classroom management, self-concept, teacher language, classroom interaction, group process, pupil outcomes, instructional concepts, learning set, role concepts, children's language, responses to literature, developmental reading, and African-American or black dialect (*Protocol Materials Catalog* 1975). McIntyre (1991) notes that 35% of universities preparing teachers use protocol materials or some variation in their preparation programs.

An extensive review of research on protocol materials is presented by Cruickshank and Haefele (1987). Several categories of studies have been undertaken: those that investigate the use of protocol materials on teacher behaviors, those that examine the material's effectiveness in helping teachers gain important concepts, and those conducted to determine whether teachers trained with protocol materials are better at bringing about certain kinds of K-12 pupil behavior. Among other things, the reviewers conclude that little related research has been done, and most of it suffers from weaknesses that make the results suspect. With these cautions in mind, we report the following.

- Participants believe experience with protocol materials is both positive and professionally worthwhile (Rentel 1974).
- Five of six studies report that using protocols enables participants to acquire the target concepts (Borg 1973; Gliessman

110

and Pugh 1976, 1978; Gliessman, Pugh, and Perry 1974; Kluecker 1974). However, Rentel (1974) finds that protocol materials produce no significant effect.

- Protocols appear to be equally effective with preservice and inservice teachers (Gliessman et al. 1974; Gliessman and Pugh 1976).
- Kluecker (1974) reports that a combination of microteaching and protocol training is significantly more effective in developing teachers' ability to recognize, categorize, and demonstrate desirable behaviors than is either method alone.
- Protocols that use filmed demonstrations of target concepts are significantly more effective than those that provide only names, or names and definitions (Gliessman and Pugh 1978).

The advantages of protocol materials include:

1. They permit preservice teachers to vicariously experience events or concepts of educational significance.
2. They provide controlled observation and analysis of events, thus promoting higher-order cognitive thought.
3. They encourage acquisition of knowledge and use of theory (interpretation and acquisition) related to the event or concept.
4. They discourage over-dependency on personal experience and bias when reacting to life in classrooms.

The major disadvantages of protocol materials are:

1. There is no consensus on the events of educational significance for which teachers should be prepared. Thus we do not have a firm foundation on which to develop protocols.
2. They are relatively expensive to develop and time-consuming to use.

Research on the effects of protocols is limited, but mostly consistent. When teachers are presented with a recording of an educational event or phenomenon and accompanying related theoretical knowledge, they develop greater conceptual understanding. Using protocols in combination with other forms of laboratory experience broadens their effect and results in greater conceptual understanding and, often, a desirable change of behavior. However, there is no evidence to indicate that this conceptual understanding and change in behavior are transferred to natural classroom settings.

Reflective Teaching

Reflective Teaching (RT) is a program that permits preservice teachers to engage in the complete act of teaching. During Reflective Teaching (Cruickshank 1991) participants plan lessons, teach them to peers, assess student learning and satisfaction, and most important, reflect or give thoughtful consideration to that act of teaching and all its attendant dimensions and subtleties. Thus its primary goal is to help preservice teachers become reflective practitioners and "students of teaching" (Cruickshank 1987).

For RT, preservice teachers are organized into groups of four to six. One member of each group is designated the teacher. These "designated teachers" are assigned a lesson and given information about the objectives of the lesson and lesson content. In a subsequent class, the designated teachers teach their 10- to 15-minute lesson to their peer groups; afterward they assess both student learning and satisfaction. The teachers and their learners then participate in small-group and then whole-class discussion. These discussions often focus on the lesson objectives and how the lesson was planned to accomplish them, what other factors influenced how instruction occurred, how well the various teaching methods used by the several designated teachers succeeded, how the learners felt about the experience, and particularly, what was learned or rediscovered about teaching and learning.

The Reflective Teaching Lessons (RTLs) are central to the Reflective Teaching method. Currently there are 41 RTLs (Cruickshank 1991). Each lesson meets five criteria:

1. It must be interesting to teach and to learn.
2. The content must be novel, that is, different from the usual academic or professional education curriculum.

3. The lesson must be brief enough to be taught successfully in 15 minutes or less.
4. The outcomes must be directly observable and measurable.
5. The lesson must be self-contained and must include all materials necessary for instruction.

A sample of RTL titles includes: "The Chisanbop Task" (a Korean method of computation that uses fingers and hands as calculators), "The Origami Task" (Japanese paper folding), and "The Good Teacher Task" (attributes of effective teachers).

Critical to the effectiveness of RT are the reflective sessions and the questions asked during them. Specifically, the aim is to ask questions that cause participants to think about teaching and learning so that they will become wiser and more thoughtful teachers. Consequently, participants may be pushed to become more aware of the determinants of their teaching behavior, more open-minded and less opinionated, more able to appreciate the perspectives of diverse learners, or more aware of the complexity of the teaching environment. Although the questions originally used in RT were developed without benefit of research, their value was substantiated later (Cruickshank, Kennedy, Williams, Holton, and Fay 1981).

Reflective Teaching is well-accepted as an on-campus laboratory experience, as demonstrated by the large distribution of the materials by Phi Delta Kappa. Phi Delta Kappa recently released a second edition of the RT materials and also conducts seminars for teacher educators who wish to become familiar with the process.

The research on Reflective Teaching has been conducted solely with preservice teachers. They find RT to be a positive experience, valuable to their professional development, more satisfying than other aspects of their methods courses, and at least as satisfying as microteaching (Bainer and Cantrell 1992; McKee 1986; Peters 1980; Peters and Moore 1980; Williams and Kennedy 1980). The experience appears significantly to promote preservice teachers' ability to analyze their own and others' teaching (Cruickshank,

Kennedy, et al. 1981; Holton and Nott 1980; Troyer 1988). Furthermore, preservice teachers report that RT reduces their anxiety about student teaching (Cruickshank, Kennedy, et al. 1981; Williams and Kennedy 1980). Beeler, Kayser, Matzner, and Saltmarsh (1985) report that RT is most successful when: 1) group size is between 5-8 and groups are heterogeneous, 2) group membership is rotated from lesson to lesson, and 3) immediate, non-threatening feedback is provided by the instructor.

A criticism of RT has been that it might promote only low level, technical reflection. However, this appears not to be the case. Kercheval (1994) finds that most post-teaching reflective sessions are not focused on the procedures used by the teachers or on the effectiveness of their teaching. Rather, issues tended to be related to the nature of teaching, how learning can be assessed, and why teachers teach as they do. Bainer and Cantrell (1992, 1994) also find that reflection following Reflective Teaching is not limited to the technical aspects of teaching or even to the stated objectives of the RTL. Rather, "the reflection exhibited thinking about both procedural aspects of teaching (*how* to teach) *and* considerations of the psychological, ethical, and social issues and consequences associated with teaching and learning (*what* and *why* to teach)" (pp. 74-75). Research by Troyer (1988) verifies that RT promotes high levels of reflection, which can be further enhanced when the experience is preceded by a session informing participants of the process and importance of reflection. In her experimental study, Troyer found both RT and RT augmented with instruction on reflection to have substantial effects on preservice teachers' reflectivity in analyzing classroom teaching.

A number of benefits of Reflective Teaching are suggested by Cruickshank (1985). They include:

1. It allows students to teach complete lessons on-campus.
2. It encourages them to try out their personal teaching style.
3. It enables them to assess their ability to bring about learning and satisfaction.
4. It allows them to reflect on their teaching and the teaching of others, with the intention of generating higher-order think-

114

ing about teaching and learning (analysis, evaluation, problem solving).

5. It occurs in a psychologically safe setting, on campus.
6. It is inexpensive.
7. It is enjoyed by preservice teachers, because they prefer learning by doing or experiential education.
8. It satisfies a need for more on-campus laboratory work.
9. It can be used in a variety of courses.

Reflective Teaching does require preservice teachers to prepare thoroughly and thoughtfully, which is time-consuming. In addition, it is threatening to those who would prefer not to have their peers see them teach. And it can be sobering when a preservice teacher discovers that when he or she teaches, learners may not learn very well or not be satisfied.

Reflective Teaching permits participants to teach, to determine learner achievement and satisfaction, and to examine the experience in a way that develops good habits of thought and teacher wisdom. And preservice teachers, their mentors, and professional organizations have seen RT to be beneficial.

Simulations

A major purpose of creating a simulation is to provide people with an opportunity to interact with some real-life phenomenon. Many things have been simulated for national defense, business, entertainment, and educational purposes. For example, astronauts have used simulators to prepare themselves to land on the moon, and high school students have used them to experience the perils of driving an automobile. Preservice teachers can use simulations to practice resolving classroom problems.

Kersh (1963) was among the first to see the application of simulations to teacher preparation. Prior to simulations being used, preservice teachers often relied on hearing their professors recount occasional "war stories" about classroom life. What they needed were opportunities to experience important aspects of the classroom in a life-like but safe setting.

Most simulations used in teacher education are intended to familiarize preservice teachers with the functions and tasks they will perform and the problems they will need to resolve. Usually, simulations: 1) present the participant with information about a hypothetical K-12 classroom, school, or pupils; 2) introduce a task or problem in the context of that simulated setting; 3) require the participant to generate one or more alternatives for performing the task or resolving the problem; and 4) provide the participant with feedback on the appropriateness of his or her effort.

The early simulations generally were media-based (film, videotape, slides, etc.) and often recreated a classroom or school and, in varying degrees of detail, provided information about students, parents, professional colleagues, and classroom. *Mr. Smith's Sixth Grade*, developed by Kersh (1963), was the first such simulator. This "Classroom Simulator" is a specially constructed mock classroom in which an elementary education student teacher, following orientation to a hypothetical school and sixth-grade classroom, is shown up to 60 filmed classroom problems. After each problem is presented, the student teacher is asked to act out or talk out a response. An experimenter then projects a "most likely" class or student reaction to the response for the student teacher to see. The intention of the simulation is to shape a student teacher's behavior in ways that juries of master teachers feel are beneficial.

Two other early simulations were the *Teacher Problems Laboratory* (TPL), developed under a U.S. Office of Education Cooperative Research Grant at the State University of New York College at Brockport (Cruickshank, Broadbent, and Bubb 1967), and the *Inner-City Simulation Laboratory* (ICSL), developed at the University of Tennessee and Ohio State University (Cruickshank 1969). In each simulation, the participant takes the role of Pat (Patrick or Patricia) Taylor, a teacher in the school, and receives realistic information about the district, school, other teachers, students, and so forth. Over the next several class sessions, participants are presented with short films, written incidents, and role plays that depict problems that have been reported by teachers to be frequent and bothersome. After each problem is presented, Pat Taylor must: 1) identify and define the problem, 2) identify factors that seem to be contributing to the problem, 3) locate pertinent information, 4) project alternative courses of action, 5) select the course of action with the fewest negative side effects, and 6) communicate or implement a decision. Following 15 to 20 minutes of independent problem solving using the materials provided, the several Pat Taylors interact with each other in both small-group and whole-class discussion, presenting their individual perspectives and solutions for inspection and critical reaction.

More recent simulations have used computers. However, the process used in these simulations is not unlike that in the earlier ones. For example, Woods, Combs, and Swan (1985-86) developed a computer-based simulation for the preparation of teachers working with emotionally or behaviorally handicapped children. In this simulation, participants receive information about each of five children, including school records, assessment reports, and the students' individualized educational plans. The participant next is presented with several problems or tasks. Using the available information, participants plan a daily schedule for each student, develop themes that are likely to be motivating, arrange the classroom, and conduct other instructional tasks. Following each task, the participant receives feedback on the decisions and is allowed to "try again" if desired.

Simulations have been well-accepted by the teacher education community (Johnson 1968; Joyce et al. 1977; Sherwin 1974). Many of the simulations available for use in teacher preparation are reviewed in Cruickshank (1988).

The research on media-based simulators has been conducted almost solely with preservice teachers and supports the notion that short-term teacher behavior can be changed through the simulation experience. Kersh (1963) and Vlcek (1966) report the Classroom Simulator causes significant and desirable changes in teacher behavior in the simulated setting. Investigations of other simulations by Anderson (1977), Cruickshank and Broadbent

(1968), Harvey (1970), and Kidder and Guthrie (1971) similarly report that participants behave in more desirable ways. Smith (1975) and Marsh (1979) indicate that simulation participants' attitudes are positively affected. Cruickshank and Broadbent (1968) note that student teachers who participate in a classroom simulation have fewer classroom problems than do those who do not participate; however, they are no more confident or positive about teaching, nor is their classroom performance visibly different. Gaffga (1967) reports that performance in the simulation is a better predictor of performance in later student teaching than are the ratings projected by mentoring education professors.

Research on computer-based simulations found that participants believe that computer simulation experiences are valuable and that computer simulations significantly affect teachers' use of desirable questioning behaviors (Woods, Combs, and Swan 1985-86). Research also has found that computer simulations affect teachers' general classroom behavior (Sitko and Semmel 1976) and ability to place students appropriately for reading instruction (Morine-Dershimer 1987). However, Morine-Dershimer found participation in the simulation to cause no significant change in teachers' beliefs about desirable instructional practices.

Kidder and Guthrie (1971) report that the effect of a simulation is significantly enhanced when participants are helped to reflect on the experience and then repeat the simulation. Interestingly, Kersh (1963) reports that the verisimilitude of media-based materials is not a factor in the effectiveness of the simulator. In fact, Kersh notes that small, still projections are somewhat more effective than are large, moving pictures in producing desirable change in teacher behavior.

When used in conjunction with student teaching or as an on-campus laboratory experience, simulations have the following advantages:

1. They permit student teachers to work toward the resolution of problems of beginning teachers that normally may not surface during student teaching because of the presence of a mentor teacher.

2. They offer opportunities for student teachers to work together to resolve problems they will encounter and to share and reflect on the possible actions and attendant values.
3. They permit the early identification of potential student teacher needs so that they might be addressed and remedied.
4. Preservice teachers can make mistakes in a safe environment.

When used in conjunction with courses in foundational studies and in teaching and learning theory courses, simulations offer additional advantages.

1. They permit study of an educational setting — neighborhood, school, and classroom — in the manner of a behavioral scientist, that is, one who observes, describes, analyzes, and attempts to understand.
2. They encourage preservice teachers to apply what they have learned in professional education courses to life in classrooms.
3. They can substitute for unstructured field experiences in schools and classrooms where the purposes and outcomes may be unclear.
4. They permit identification of preservice teachers who by temperament or preparation may not be well suited for student teaching or teaching at all.

Among the disadvantages of simulations are:

1. They are not real situations, thus participants may not take their roles seriously.
2. They require college instructors who can guide preservice teachers in identifying and applying theoretical knowledge to life in classrooms; and
3. They usually contain many components and therefore require special handling and care.

Simulations provide safe, controlled opportunities for preservice teachers to learn about many facets of life in classrooms.

They can acquaint preservice teachers with almost any aspect of school or classroom reality. The simulations used most frequently permit preservice teachers to practice solving classroom problems and applying theory.

Recommendations

Instruction within teacher preparation still is dominated by a few traditional ways of teaching and embellished by extensive use of field experiences. However, a few persons have given considerable time and serious thought to how else preservice teachers might be taught. Unfortunately, attention to the results of their efforts has been scant and short-lived.

Fortunately, the value of the above six alternative ways to teach is rediscovered from time to time. What is needed is study of what education professors know about those six alternatives, their reactions to their purposes and procedures, and to what extent and how they use them. Following this recommendation, we would add these:

1. All instructional alternatives that can be used in teacher preparation should be identified and categorized according to the purposes they could serve.
2. Related instructional materials also should be identified and made available for use in teacher preparation programs.
3. Students preparing to become teacher educators should be knowledgeable about and skilled in using a variety of instructional alternatives. However, the six alternatives examined in this chapter should receive special attention.
4. Additional means should constantly be sought for delivering the teacher preparation curriculum more suitably.

We have given too little attention to the instruction or teaching of teachers. Perhaps our greatest contribution can be through modeling or practicing what we preach, and teaching as well as we know how.

References

Allen, D., and Ryan, K. *Microteaching.* Reading, Mass.: Addison-Wesley, 1969.

Anderson, R. "A Simulation Game Designed to Teach Group Member Roles to Prospective Teachers." Paper presented at the annual meeting of the American Educational Research Association, New York, April 1977. ERIC Document Reproduction Service No. ED 135 870.

Argyris, C. "Some Limitations of the Case Method: Experiences in a Management Development Program." *Academy of Management Review* 5, no. 2 (1980): 291-98.

Bainer, D.L., and Cantrell, D. "Nine Dominant Reflection Themes Identified for Preservice Teachers by a Content Analysis of Essays." *Education* 112, no. 4 (1992): 571-78.

Bainer, D.L., and Cantrell, D. "The Relationship Between Instructional Domain and the Content of Reflection Among Preservice Teachers." *Teacher Education Quarterly* 20, no 4 (1994): 65-76.

Becler, K.; Kayser, G.; Matzner, K.; and Saltmarsh, R. "Reflective Teaching: Reflections on College Classroom Experience." *Educational Journal* 18, no. 1 (1985): 4-8.

Berliner, D. "Laboratory Settings and the Study of Teacher Education." *Journal of Teacher Education* 36, no. 6 (1985): 2-8.

Borg, W. "The Minicourse as a Vehicle for Changing Teacher Behavior: A Three Year Follow Up." *Journal of Educational Psychology* 63, no. 6 (1972): 23-30.

Borg, W. "Protocols: Competency-Based Teacher Education Modules." *Educational Technology* 13, no. 10 (1973): 17-20.

Borg, W. "Protocol Materials as Related to Teacher Performance and Pupil Achievement." *Journal of Educational Research* 69, no. 1 (1975): 23-30.

Borg, W.; Kallenbach, W.; Morris, M.; and Friebel, A. "Videotape Feedback and Microteaching in a Teacher Training Model." *Journal of Experimental Education* 37, no. 4 (1969): 9-16.

Borg, W.; Langer, P.; and Wilson, J. "Teacher Classroom Management Skills and Pupil Behavior." *Journal of Experimental Education* 37, no. 4 (1975): 9-16.

Borg, W., and Stone, D. "Protocol Materials as a Tool for Changing Teacher Behavior." *Journal of Experimental Education* 43, no. 1 (1974): 34-39.

Butler, E. "An Experimental Study of the Case Method in Teaching the Social Foundations of Education." Doctoral dissertation, University of Tennessee, 1966.

Copeland, W. "The Relationship Between Microteaching and Student Teaching Classroom Performance." *Journal of Educational Research* 68 (1975): 289-93.

Copeland, W. "Some Factors Related to Student Teacher Classroom Performance Following Microteaching Training." *American Educational Research Journal* 14, no. 2 (1977): 147-57.

Copeland, W. "Laboratory Experiences in Teacher Education." In *Encyclopedia of Educational Research,* edited by H. Mitzel. New York: Free Press, 1982.

Copeland, W., and Doyle, W. "Laboratory Skill Training and Student Teacher Classroom Performance." *Journal of Experimental Education* 42, no. 1 (1973): 16-21.

Cruickshank, D.R. *Inner-City Simulation Laboratory.* Chicago: Science Research Associates, 1969.

Cruickshank, D.R. "Uses and Benefits of Reflective Teaching." *Phi Delta Kappan* 66 (June 1985): 704-706.

Cruickshank, D.R. *Reflective Teaching: The Preparation of Students of Teaching.* Reston, Va.: Association of Teacher Educators, 1987.

Cruickshank, D.R. "The Uses of Simulations in Teacher Preparation." *Simulation and Games* 19, no. 2 (1988): 133-56.

Cruickshank, D.R. *Research that Informs Teachers and Teacher Educators.* Bloomington, Ind.: Phi Delta Kappa Educational Foundation, 1990.

Cruickshank, D.R. *Reflective Teaching.* 2nd ed. Bloomington, Ind.: Phi Delta Kappa, 1991.

Cruickshank D.R.; Bainer, D.; and Metcalf, K. *The Act of Teaching.* New York: McGraw-Hill, 1995.

Cruickshank, D.R., and Broadbent, F. "Simulation and Analysis of Problems of Beginning Teachers." *Educational Technology* 9, no. 10 (1968): 50-54.

Cruickshank, D.R.; Broadbent, F.; and Bubb, R. *The Teaching Problems Laboratory.* Chicago: Science Research Associates, 1967.

Cruickshank, D.R., and Haefele, D. "Teacher Preparation Via Protocol Materials." *International Journal of Educational Research* 11, no. 5 (1987): 543-54.

Cruickshank, D.R.; Holton, J.; Fay, D.; Williams, J.; Kennedy, J.; Myers, B.; and Hough, B. *Reflective Teaching.* Bloomington, Ind.: Phi Delta Kappa, 1981.

Cruickshank, D.R.; Kennedy, J.; Williams, J.; Holton, J.; and Fay, D. "Evaluation of Reflective Teaching Outcomes." *Journal of Educational Research* 75, no. 1 (1981): 26-32.

Evertson, C. "Bridging Knowledge and Action Through Clinical Experiences." In *What Teachers Need to Know*, edited by D. Dill. San Francisco: Jossey-Bass, 1990.

Gaffga, R. "Simulation: A Model for Observing Student Teacher Behavior." Doctoral dissertation, University of Tennessee, 1967.

Gall, M.; Dunning, B.; Banks, H.; and Galassi, J. "Comparison of Instructional Media in a Minicourse on High Cognitive Questions." Paper presented at the annual meeting of the American Educational Research Association, Chicago, April 1972. ERIC Document Reproduction Service No. ED 064 326.

Gliessman, D.; Geillo, D.; and Archer, A. "Changes in Teacher Problem-Solving: Two Studies." Paper presented at the annual meeting of the American Educational Research Association, San Francisco, April 1989.

Gliessman, D., and Pugh, R. "The Development and Evaluation of Protocol Films in Teacher Education." *AV Communications Review* 24, no. 1 (1976): 21-48.

Gliessman, D., and Pugh, R. "Research on the Rationale, Design, and Effectiveness of Protocol Materials." *Journal of Teacher Education* 29, no. 6 (1978): 87-91.

Gliessman, D.; Pugh, R.; and Perry, F. *Effects of a Protocol Film Series in Terms of Learning Outcomes and Reactions of Users*. Bloomington: Indiana University, National Center for the Development of Training Materials in Teacher Education, 1974. ERIC Document Reproduction Service No. ED 064 326.

Harrington, H. "Developing Cases for Teacher Education: Issues and Concerns." Paper presented to the American Educational Research Association, Chicago, April 1991.

Harvey, W. *A Study of the Cognitive and Effective Outcomes of a Collegiate Science Learning Game*. Tallahassee: Florida State University Computer-Assisted Instruction Center, 1970. ERIC Document Reproduction Service No. ED 050 552.

Hofmeister, A., and Stowikowski, J. *Validation of Minicourse Five for Special Education. Final Report*. Washington, D.C.: U.S. Office of Education, 1972. ERIC Document Reproduction Service No. 068 456.

Holton, J., and Nott, D. "The Experimental Effects of Reflective Teaching on Preservice Teachers' Ability to Think and Talk Critically About Teaching and Learning." Paper presented to the Educational Research Association, Boston, April 1980.

Johnson, J. *A National Survey of Student Teaching Programs*. USOE Report No. 6-8182. Washington, D.C.: U.S. Office of Education, 1968.

Joyce, B.; Yarger, S.; Howey, K.; Harbeck. K.; and Kluwin. T. *Preservice Teacher Education*. Palo Alto, Calif.: Center for Educational Research and Development, 1977.

Kallenbach, W., and Ward, B. "A Preservice/Inservice Field Test of Minicourse 15: Developing Student Independent Study Skills." Paper presented to the American Educational Research Association, Chicago, April 1974. ERIC Document Reproduction Service No. ED 090 237.

Katz, G. "Use of Minicourse Instruction with Student Teachers of Educable Mentally Retarded Children." *Journal of Educational Research* 69 (1976): 355-59.

Kercheval, A. "The Critical Role of the Laboratory Instructor During On-Campus Reflective Teaching." Paper presented to the Midwestern Educational Research Association, Chicago, October 1994.

Kersh, B. *Classroom Simulation: A New Dimension in Teacher Education*. Monmouth: Oregon State University, Oregon State System of Higher Education, Teaching Research Division, 1963. ERIC Document Reproduction Service No. ED 010 176.

Kidder, S., and Guthrie, J. *The Training Effects of a Behavioral Modification Game*. Baltimore: Johns Hopkins University, Center for the Study of Social Organization of Schools, 1971. ERIC Document Reproduction Service No ED 057 613.

Kleinfeld, J. "Changes in Problem Solving Abilities of Students Taught Through Case Methods." Paper presented to the American Educational Research Association, Chicago, 1991.

Kluecker, J. "Effects of Protocol and Training Materials." In *Acquiring Teaching Competencies: Reports and Studies, No. 6*, edited by L.D. Brown. Bloomington: Indiana University, National Center for the Development of Training Materials in Teacher Education, 1974. ERIC Document Reproduction Service No. ED 297 962.

Lawrence, P. "The Preparation of Case Material." In *The Case Method of Teaching Human Relations and Administration*, edited by K. Andrews. Cambridge, Mass.: Harvard University Press, 1953.

Leone, R. "Teaching Management Without Cases." Manuscript. Boston: Boston University School of Management, 1989.

MacLeod, G. "Microteaching: Modeling." In *The International Encyclopedia of Teaching and Teacher Education*, edited by M. Dunkin. Oxford: Pergamon, 1987.

Marsh, C. "Teacher Education Simulations: The 'Challenge of Change' Example." *British Journal of Teacher Education* 5, no. 1 (1979): 63-71.

McDonald, F. "Behavior Modification in Teacher Education." In *The Seventy-Second Yearbook of the National Society for the Study of Education, Part II,* edited by C. Thoreson. Chicago: University of Chicago Press, 1973.

McIntyre, D. "The Utilization of Laboratory Experiences in Undergraduate Teacher Education Programs." Paper presented to the Association of Teacher Educators, New Orleans, February 1991.

McKee, A. "Reflective Teaching as a Strategy in TAFE Teacher Education." Paper presented to the South Pacific Association of Teacher Educators, Perth, Australia, 1986.

Metcalf, K. "Laboratory Experiences in Teacher Education." In *The International Encyclopedia of Education,* 2nd ed., edited by T. Husen and T. Postlethwaite. Oxford: Pergamon Press, 1994.

Morine-Dershimer, G. "Creating a Recycling Center for Teacher Thinking." In *Simulation and Clinical Knowledge in Teacher Education,* edited by E. Doak, T. Hipple, and M. Keith. Knoxville: University of Tennessee, 1987.

National Association of State Directors of Teacher Education and Certification. *Standards for the State Approval of Teacher Education.* Salt Lake City: Utah State University, 1981.

Perott, E. "Minicourses." In *The International Encyclopedia of Teaching and Teacher Education,* edited by M. Dunkin. Oxford: Pergamon Press, 1987.

Peters, J. "Effects of Laboratory Teaching Experience on Students Views of Themselves as Teachers." Paper presented at the annual meeting of the National Agricultural Education Research Association, New Orleans, 1980.

Peters, J., and Moore, G. *A Comparison of Two Methods of Providing Laboratory Experience for Student Teachers in Agricultural Education.* Lafayette, Ind.: Purdue University, 1980. ERIC Document Reproduction Service No. ED 019 847.

Protocol Materials Catalog. Tallahassee: Florida State Department of Education, 1975. ERIC Document Reproduction Service No. ED 100 993.

Rector, D.; Hull, R.; and Mohan, M. *A Field Test of the Effectiveness of One of the Utah State University Protocol Training Materials in an Inservice Workshop Setting.* Fredonia: State University of New York, Teacher Education Research Center, 1972. ERIC Document Reproduction Service No. ED 075 341.

Rentel, V. "A Protocol Materials Evaluation: The Language of Children." *Journal of Teacher Education* 25, no. 4 (1974): 323-29.

Sherwin, S. *Teacher Education: A Status Report.* Princeton, N.J.: Educational Testing Service, 1974.

Sitko, M., and Semmel, M. *The Effectiveness of a Computer-Assisted Teacher Training System (CATTS) in the Development of Reading and Listening Comprehension.* Bloomington: Indiana University, Center for Innovation in Teaching the Handicapped, 1976. ERIC Document Reproduction Service No. ED 162 467.

Smith, B.; Cohen, S.; and Pearl, A. *Teachers for the Real World.* Washington, D.C.: American Association of Colleges for Teacher Education, 1969.

Smith, C. "Personality and Attitudinal Shift Under a Simulated Teaching Experience." *Improving College and University Teaching* 23, no. 4 (1975): 229-31.

Sykes, G., and Bird, T. "Teacher Education and the Case Idea." *Review of Educational Research* 18 (1992): 457-521.

Troyer, M. "The Effects of Reflective Teaching and a Supplemental Theoretical Component on Preservice Teachers' Reflectivity in Analyzing Classroom Teaching Situations." Doctoral dissertation, Ohio State University, 1988.

Vlcek, C. "Classroom Simulation in Teacher Education." *Audiovisual Instructor* 11, no. 2 (1966): 86-90.

Williams, E., and Kennedy, J. "Variations in Preservice Teachers' Mode of Reflection About Teaching According to Their Conceptual Levels and Participation in Reflective Teaching." Paper presented to the American Educational Research Association, Boston, 1980.

Winitsky, N., and Arends, R. "Translating Research into Practice: The Forms of Training and Clinical Experience on Preservice Students' Knowledge, Reflectivity, and Behavior." *Journal of Teacher Education* 42, no. 1 (1991): 52-65.

Woods, M.; Combs, C.; and Swan, W. "Computer Simulations: Field Testing Effectiveness and Efficiency for Inservice and Preservice Teacher Preparation." *Journal of Educational Technology Systems* 14, no. 1 (1985-86): 61-74.

Related Readings

Allen, D.; Bush, R.; Ryan, K.; and Cooper, J. *Teaching Skills for Elementary and Secondary Teachers.* New York: General Learning, 1969.

Berliner, D. "Impediments to the Study of Teacher Effectiveness." *Journal of Teacher Education* 27, no. 1 (1976): 5-14.

Gage, N. "A Factorially Designed Experiment on Teacher Structuring, Soliciting and Reacting." *Journal of Teacher Education* 27, no. 1 (1976): 35-39.

Joncich-Clifford, G., and Guthrie, J. *Ed School.* Chicago: University of Chicago Press, 1988.

McKnight, P. "Development of the Technical Skills of Teaching, 1968-1978 and Beyond." Paper presented to the American Educational Research Association, April 1978. ERIC Document Reproduction Service No. ED 171 699.

Peterson, P.; Marx, R.; and Clark, C. "Teacher Planning, Teacher Behavior and Student Achievement." *American Educational Research Journal* 15, no. 3 (1978): 417-32.

Risko, V.; Yount, D.; and Towell, J. "Video-Based Case Analysis to Enhance Teacher Preparation." Paper presented to the College Reading Association, 1990.

Roe, M.F., and Stillman, A.C. "A Comparative Study of Dialogue and Response Journals." *Teaching and Teacher Education* 10, no. 6 (1994): 579-88.

Chapter 4
REFORMING TEACHER EDUCATION: PREDICTABLE FAILURE OR OUR ONLY HOPE

The goal of teacher education is to prepare the very best teachers for America's schools. In support of that goal are a strong curricular tradition, a large number of ideas for curriculum reform, and a variety of instructional alternatives for preparing teachers.

Nevertheless, teacher education also has been the target of recurrent, strong criticism. The critics of teacher education have come from both inside and outside the profession. For example, John Silber, president of Boston University, has said, "There is no way we can begin with a talent pool that is below average and end up with a cadre of teachers capable of upgrading our public schools" (Lewis and Lewis 1990). And Lynne Cheney (1990), former chairperson of the National Endowment for the Humanities, has criticized teacher preparation for, among other things: not being a separate discipline with a distinct body of knowledge, teaching courses that are intellectually demeaning, and using dull textbooks.

People inside the profession also criticize teacher education. Lynn Olson (1990), a reporter for *Education Week*, reported some of the concerns of teacher educators:

- Teacher preparation is not in tune with practice in K-12 schools.
- Teacher education is not intellectually solid; it lacks a knowledge base.
- The preparation curriculum is not coherent.

- The curriculum does not focus sufficiently on special methods of teaching ("pedagogical content knowledge").
- Teacher educators cannot explain why they are doing what they are doing.
- There are too few professional courses.
- Preservice teachers are not adequately prepared to manage classrooms.
- Preservice teachers do not learn how to be reflective.
- Preservice teachers' initial beliefs about education and teaching go unchallenged.
- Teacher educators do not model a variety of teaching techniques.
- Teacher educators avoid discussing teaching and the preparation curriculum.
- Teacher educators do not use such promising instructional alternatives as cases or simulations to introduce preservice teachers to the common problems in K-12 classes.

Criticism often can drive reform, and such criticism should be examined carefully. This has not happened in teacher education. Indeed, there seem to be strong obstacles to reform in teacher education.

Olson suggests that the obstacles to reform in teacher preparation are underfunding, a lack of genuine interest throughout the university, and overly prescriptive state regulations for the preparation curriculum and instruction.

Bush (1987), who developed microteaching at Stanford University, identifies 25 reform reports dating to 1929. He concludes that reform largely has been ineffectual because:

- There are too many stakeholders sharing power in teacher preparation, each holding a different perspective.
- There is a lack of sufficient space in the teacher preparation curriculum to include what teachers need to know and be able to do.
- There is a belief that there must be one best way to prepare teachers.
- Teacher education is underfunded.

In *The Predictable Failure of Educational Reform*, Seymour Sarason asks two fundamental questions: Why have the recommendations of task forces and committees consistently been ineffective? and, Is reform doomed to failure? Sarason answers the second question with a qualified Yes; reform efforts will fail unless all stakeholders recognize who and what schools are for ("fostering the desire to continue to learn about self, others, and the world"), and unless they understand and confront the obstacles that have stopped reform from succeeding. Sarason suggests that the obstacles are: failure to understand and change the existing power relationships among stakeholders, failure of internal and external stakeholders to understand each other's needs, the belief that education institutions can solve serious social problems, and unrealistic reform timetables (such as the Goal 2000: Educate America Act timetable for massive change).

There are at least a dozen critical impediments to reform in teacher preparation. They are:

1. *Political territorialism.* There are a large number of stakeholders with quite different values and priorities and vested interests — for example, state education departments, universities, teacher organizations, teacher education organizations, the federal government, local education agencies, and business and industry.

2. *Conflicting ideologies.* Teacher educators often hold conflicting beliefs regarding the ends and means of both schooling and teacher preparation, and these beliefs can affect reform efforts (Iannone 1976; Zeichner 1983; Zeichner and Liston 1990).

3. *Lack of vision.* There are teacher educators who have no vision of the reality of schooling and who are out of step with prevailing concepts.

4. *Lack of space.* There is little, if any, room in professional education to accommodate reform ideas.

5. *Limited resources.* Universities seem to have little regard for teacher preparation; thus schools of education "are the

lowest funded in the university and that they have lost ground over the past ten years in terms of constant dollars and in relation to other disciplines" (Ebmeier et al. 1991, p. 233).

6. *Lack of accountability*. Seldom is anyone held directly accountable for implementing, maintaining, and evaluating teacher preparation reform ideas.

7. *Lack of staff development*. Teacher educators have little knowledge of and experience with specific reform programs. Consequently, reforms may be poorly implemented.

8. *Voluntary participation*. Implementing a reform in a school of education almost always is optional, that is, each teacher educator can make a choice about whether to use the reform ideas.

9. *Fickleness*. Teacher educators seem almost eager to be distracted from one buzzword or idea to another;

10. *Doubtfulness*. Teacher educators may just doubt that the proposed reform is valid.

11. *Loose coupling with schools*. Teachers in K-12 schools may be either unable or reluctant to reinforce reform in teacher preparation. Local teachers do not perceive themselves as teacher educators, and they often have little time for or interest in that endeavor, except periodically to accept student teachers.

12. *Complacency*. Teacher educators share with mankind in general a preference for the comfort of the status quo as against the uncomfortable possibilities of unknown, untried programs.

Teacher educators must become more active with regard to criticism and attendant reform ideas. If teacher educators do not take the responsibility, outside stakeholders will; and such forced reforms may not lead to the betterment of teacher preparation. Witness such events as state legislators reducing professional preparation in Texas and Virginia.

Teacher educators must be part of the solution, rather than part of the problem. Thus they must:

1. Continue to examine the various criticisms of teacher education and determine their validity.
2. When a criticism is found to be valid, teacher educators must find ways to correct the problem.
3. Determine what may interfere with implementing a promising reform and eliminate that impediment.

Unless teacher educators accept such professional responsibility, teacher preparation will become professionally bankrupt. We never have lacked ideas for the reform of teacher preparation, but we have sorely lacked the consensus, focus, moxie, and persistence to carry them through.

References

Bush, R.M. "Teacher Education Reform: Lessons from the Past." *Journal of Teacher Education* 38 (May-June 1987): 13-19.

Cheney, L. *Tyrannical Machines: A Report on Educational Practices Gone Wrong and Our Best Hopes for Setting Them Right*. Washington, D.C.: National Endowment for the Humanities, 1990.

Ebmeier, H.; Twombly, S.; and Teeter, D. "The Comparability and Adequacy of Financial Support for Schools of Education." *Journal of Teacher Education* 42, no. 3 (1991): 226-35.

Iannone, R. "Current Orientations in Teacher Education." In *Handbook on Contemporary Education*, edited by S. Goodman. New York: Xerox, 1976.

Lewis, C., and Lewis, S. "The Failure of Teacher Education." *Newsweek*, 1 October 1990, pp. 58-60.

Olson, L. "Teaching Our Teachers." *Education Week*, 12 December 1990, pp. 11-15, 20-21, 24-26.

Sarason, S. *The Predictable Failure of Educational Reform*. San Francisco: Jossey-Bass, 1990.

Zeichner, K. "Alternative Paradigms of Teacher Education." *Journal of Teacher Education* 34, no. 3 (1983): 3-9.

Zeichner, K., and Liston, D. "Traditions of Reform in U.S. Teacher Education." *Journal of Teacher Education* 41, no. 2 (1990): 3-20.